THE STORM

A Poetry Collection for the Broken Hearted

To all those who have fallen confused to their knees,
just trying to stand up again.
-Lindsey Kay Atkinson

LINDSEY KAY ATKINSON

authorHOUSE

AuthorHouse™
1663 Liberty Drive
Bloomington, IN 47403
www.authorhouse.com
Phone: 833-262-8899

© 2021 Lindsey Kay Atkinson. All rights reserved.

No part of this book may be reproduced, stored in a retrieval system, or transmitted by any means without the written permission of the author.

Published by AuthorHouse 06/02/2021

ISBN: 978-1-6655-2652-4 (sc)
ISBN: 978-1-6655-2650-0 (hc)
ISBN: 978-1-6655-2651-7 (e)

Library of Congress Control Number: 2021910219

Print information available on the last page.

Any people depicted in stock imagery provided by Getty Images are models, and such images are being used for illustrative purposes only.
Certain stock imagery © Getty Images.

This book is printed on acid-free paper.

Because of the dynamic nature of the Internet, any web addresses or links contained in this book may have changed since publication and may no longer be valid. The views expressed in this work are solely those of the author and do not necessarily reflect the views of the publisher, and the publisher hereby disclaims any responsibility for them.

CONTENTS

Note From The Author ix

❖ **The Hurt. The Pain. The Heartbreak.**
This, To Myself 1
Empty Promises 3
Shower Thoughts 5
Denied 7
Fire 10
Ice 11
Pattern 13
Yet Again 14
Vicious Cycle 16
Stayed 17
Momma 19
I Told You So 21
Ice Cream 22
Last Time 23
Wasted 25
Skeletons 26
Mirage 28
Glass House 29
God Sent 31
Thirsty 32
Had Me Convinced 34
Pity Her 36
Past 38
Trash 39
Forgive, Than To Forget 40
Expectations 42
Actually Loved Me 43
Gamble 44
Too Late 45
Season 46

❖ **Dirty Laundry & Memories To Burn**
Pictures Of Her 51
In Love With Her 53

Her Things 56
Ultimatum 59
Could Sleep 62
Third Heart 65
Misled 67
Got Away 69
Map 72
Guilty 74
Complacent 75
Home Wrecker 79
Hope She's Happy 83
Quid Pro Quo 85
Necklace 87
Prisoner 92
Screaming Match 94
Record Of Wrong 96
Fooled 100
Exhausting 101
I Knew This 102
Pieces 104
Shadows 110
One-Way 113
Ruined Us 115
Bully 118
Closed Doors 121
Publicity 122
Hike 128
Villain 132

❖ Apologies & Regretful Reminisces

Your Person 135
Bed 137
Heartbreaker 138
Sacrificed 140
Jaws 141
Dead 144
War 151
Pride 153
Fear 155

Slip Away	156
Pyramid	158
Poison	160
Cry	162
Girls	165
Gone	168

❖ Starting Over & Moving On

Fly	175
Refuel	177
Dinner For One	178
Swallow	179
For Good	181
Why Not	183
Victim	184
I Wasn't	186
Out Of Sight Out Of Mind	188
Curse	189
Just Getting Started	190
Daily Dose	192
Second Chances	195
Hypocrite	197
Leave	200
Pros And Cons	201
Body Language	204
Think, That Way	206
2:00 A.M. Thoughts	208
First Impressions	209
Which Shoulder	211
Happily Ever After	213
Me	217
Feet On The Ground	219
Storms	225

Dear Reader	**229**
Acknowledgements	**231**
About The Author	**233**
Books Coming Soon	**235**

NOTE FROM THE AUTHOR

Most of those who have been around for my relationships, never knew what actually went on behind closed doors. Anyone who may have been observing from the outside in, would've been missing many parts of the story. Yet they always felt obligated to encourage me to stay and 'fight for love'.

Well, I always chose to fight for love, not because I was told, but because I always felt like I could truly save someone's heart. Love them back to feeling complete.

Over the years with this mindset, I lost myself. I lost my self worth, and honestly, it's not our job to convince people to love us. Those who deserve our time and attention, just should. Without being told, and without being reminded to.

What happens when the love you're in, you realize is completely lost, and only you know it?

Only you feel it? Do you leave, or do you stay and try to save it?

You're most likely reading this book, because like me, your choice was ALWAYS to stay and fight. Your choice was to fight for a love you truly believed in, and in doing so, you got burned pretty bad in the process. That's okay.

Every pain is a lesson, every lesson is a growth, and we should always want to continue growing.

With no one unbiased to turn to during all of my struggles and heartbreak, I decided to write. Within these pages are some of my most painful memories and experiences from the last decade of my life, all shared amongst 12 different women. These are their stories. *DING DING*

[If you got that SVU reference, you're my kind of person.]

THE HURT.
THE PAIN.
THE HEARTBREAK.

This, To Myself

I only know how to love one way.
Vulnerably.

My shirt sleeves
are starting to get baggy
from all the years
of wearing such a heavy
heart on them.

But that's all I know
how to do.
Stitch it back up
after it falls for another
and breaks again.

Oooo, she looks good....safe.

"Hello. Here you go!
My most prized red possession!
I know it looks worn,
battered.
It is.
But I promise it still works,
look watch...

...oh, you don't want it either?"

Maybe something
is wrong with it?
It's been broken many times, but...
...I thought I fixed it?

I thought,
this time
would be different.

It's unique you see,
so unique
that I can't actually buy
replacement pieces for it.

I could reach out
to the many others
that took a piece of mine
with them,
but, I can't.

You see,
they took the small of mine
with them,
and stitched it up
with theirs when they fixed it,
and well,
then they gave it
away to another.

I don't know
who has it now…
All I know is that I,
don't.

Well, now
I just feel broken again,
and there's no one
to blame
for this pain,
because I keep doing **this**,
to myself.

Empty Promises

They're always so sure,
when they leave.

That I'm not what
they want.
Not what they
signed up for.

The problem with this,
is that I've already
imprinted on them.

They know me.
My heart, my intentions,
all the good parts.
Those good parts, well,
they're not easily forgotten.

I'm now a part of them,
a part of their story,
and I've embedded myself
into their memory forever,
whether they like it or not.

I left my mark of passion
on their soul.
I left my mark of love
in their heart.

They think about me
from time to time randomly,
and without any warning
that it's coming.

Memories don't care
where you're at,
how old you are,
or who you're standing next to
when it hits.
It just hits.
Really hard sometimes.

It makes them miss me.
Some, even reach out
to tell me so.

They sometimes crawl back,
with a basket of apologies
and "I'm sorry's" during these
moments of weakness,
but I see through it.

I'm kind of cold now,
but not completely heartless.

I'm kind of quiet now,
but not completely silent.

I'm kind of guarded now,
but not completely closed off.

I can see through their words
like an open window
on a clear summer's day.

They can no longer fool me,
and they are no longer
in control of me.

I have forgiven them,
but I will never forget
their abundance
of **empty promises.**

Shower Thoughts

I place my palms
on the cold, stoned, wall
and let the luke warm water
run down my spine.

It's not until
I close my eyes,
that I can feel
the ghost presence
of where her hands
once called home.

I bow my head slowly,
and can feel the traced route
they used to take.

From the tops of my traps,
to the back of my shoulders,
down to mid spine
and then locked around my torso.

There it was,
my favorite part.
Her warm cheek
pressed tightly to my back.
We were locked in
and I felt safe.

I wanted her to never,
let me go.

My face was soaked,
so I lifted my head
and opened my eyes.

Lindsey Kay Atkinson

There I was,
yet again,
back to reality,
and thought to myself,

'I should probably
turn on
the water,
and drown out
the sound
of my **shower thoughts.**'

Denied

I never thought
that I'd grow up
to be someone with
such good self-esteem
and confidence.

I also never expected
that one day
I'd lose that.

People you allow
into your life,
can either
build your confidence
back up to where it
deserves to be,
or they can completely,
disintegrate it.

Girl after a girl,
relationship after relationship,
if I wanted it,
I got it,
and the trick to hook them
was my confidence.

After all,
confidence is sexy.
The only problem was,
it was all
false confidence.

They didn't fall in love
with my insecurities.

They didn't fall in love
with my trust issues.

They didn't fall in love
with the fact that I
didn't love myself,
or my body.

How could they,
when it was always
kept hidden behind
the charming smiles,
late night conversations,
and distracting jokes?

But the problem with
false confidence,
is that the ugly truth
will eventually
reveal itself.

This year I'm 28,
and it's honestly
the first time
anyone has ever
denied me.

I immediately regretted
the confessions of
my insecurities,
and I immediately felt
shame for telling the truth about
my trust issues
and who I am now
because of them.

Until I quickly realized
that who it was
that was getting denied in

that moment,
IS who I am,
every single day
that I wake up.

I always got my way
and who I wanted
because it wasn't me.
Not all of me anyway.

I was giving them
someone they didn't know.

I was giving them
the version of myself
that honestly,
even I hated
deep down inside.

I would take mental notes
of what these women
said they wanted,
what they said they liked,
and who they found attractive.

In doing this
I guess I would
subconsciously morph
into that dream person for them,
and inevitably
set myself up for failure
time and time again
when I couldn't keep up the act.

I will forever be grateful
for the lesson I learned,
to just be myself, always,
and for the day I got **denied**.

Fire

I miss the warmth
of her touch.

The burn
in her kiss.

How she was so good
at blanketing me
with comfort and security
in every word.

With the blink of her eyes
in my direction,
I would melt
in the palms
of her hands.

Fully surrendering
to anything
and everything
she wanted and needed
from me.

Baby,
what happened to us?
We're a pile of ash,
where we used to be,
fire.

Ice

Some days she was here,
and others she was not.

Physically always,
but not mentally.

Some days,
she was so cold
and distant,
I could see my breath
when I spoke to her.

Her behavior
on days like this
were misleading.

When before,
she'd open up to me
like a flower in the spring,
now she froze
when I'd ask her to tell me
how she was feeling.

I wondered
if she'd purposefully choose
which days to feel like this?

Why were they getting
more and more frequent?

She'd go from
being short,
to being silent.

Then I'd feel like
I had to pull teeth
just to get her emotions
to scratch the surface
like an ice pick
on the cube
she'd put her
heart in.

I wanted her to
hold onto me,
and let me
thaw her out.

To feel me,
and the warmth
of my love for her.

To give in,
and let me crack
the core
wide open,
breaking through
the **ice**.

Pattern

I hoped to always
be enough for her.

I prayed that the love
her and I thought
we'd found,
would stay forever,
and never,
fizzle out.

But no matter how much
I gave,
she was always
craving
and seeking more.

After all,
that's how we met.

I was more than they were
for her,
at the time,
and I had won over
her heart.

But only
for the moment.

I don't know what
made me believe
that **pattern**,
would stop with me.

Yet Again

Laying in bed,
alone and cold,
I continue to torture myself
by replaying
the entire relationship
in my head
over and over.

It's like a poorly made movie,
so bad
that I can't stand
to watch another second of it.

Yet here I am,
glued
and unable to look away.

I can't even enjoy
the good parts anymore,
because even those now,
bring sadness
and make me cry.

I've cried so hard
and for so long,
that I feel blind.
Dry.

My first thought
is that I'll be okay,
because she'll come
rushing to my side,
to nurse me
back to health.

The Storm

But lately
I am living
in an abandoned hospital,
and the windows
to my soul
refuse,
to stop leaking.

I can't help it,
as the feeling of
misery
trickles back into
these empty
hallways of my heart,
yet again.

Vicious Cycle

The more I swept things under the rug,
the less we'd resolve our issues.

The less we'd resolve our issues,
the more we'd fight.

The more we'd fight,
the less loved I'd feel.

The less loved I'd feel,
the more I'd shut down.

The more I'd shut down,
the less they'd check in on me.

The less they'd check in on me,
the more distant we got.

The more distant we got,
the less we spoke.

The less we spoke,
the more leaning towards
breaking up
we became.

Now we're both single,
because we never
figured out
how to break
the **vicious cycle.**

Stayed

I didn't leave,
because she had
convinced me
that it was finally over.

The pain,
the heartache,
the endings,
the starting overs.

I didn't leave,
despite the number
of fights and arguments
because I made her
a promise.

One that I intended
to keep, forever.

I didn't leave,
through the ups and downs
and the "I don't know what I want" moments,
because I had
convinced myself
that I could help her
figure it all out.

She verbally,
physically,
and mentally
abused me
time and time again.

Belittle was now a word
so commonly used
that I wore it, confused,
but pinned to my shirt
like a prized accomplishment.

She made me feel
less than desirable
and unloved
everyday.

But I loved her.
Truly loved her.

And that's all I could
ever feel,
in those moments.

She pushed
further and further away
until she could
call herself,
"free".

And still,
looking back,
I know I would've
stayed.

Momma

As a little girl,
I never liked playing with dolls
or dressing up.

I never liked boys, but
I've always wanted to be
a mom.

"Lesbians can't have kids!"
"How are you going to manage that?!"
they'd say.

Hopeless.

Maybe they're right?
Maybe everyone's not cut out
to be a mom?

But I just can't…

Can't get the images out of my head.

He's with blurred face,
just a shadow of a
memory tucked far away
from another lifetime,
but I can still see him.

I can see him swinging,
because I'm who's pushing him
to different heights.

I can hear him,
giggling and laughing
"higher momma higher!"

I can smell him,
freshly shampooed
and ready to be tucked in
before I leave for work.

I can feel him,
Jesus that is,
present with the two of us
kneeled at the foot of his bed
for prayer.

I can see him,
and all the love
he has for me
in every canvas painting
he has ever made
for me to keep.

I remember him,
and I will forever be grateful
for these memories.

One day,
I will be a mom,
and until then
my heart will forever be
with the boy
who first called me
"**Momma**".

I Told You So

Why is it
that when our heads
know better,
our hearts
don't want to listen?

Why is it
that when our hearts
get hurt,
our head
suddenly stays quiet?

Why is it
that when our head
stays quiet,
our gut
has nothing better to say
other than,
"I told you so."

Ice Cream

I no longer want
to be her
late night
ice cream snack.

Where she'd take me
out of hiding
in the dark of night
and make me
melt in the palms
of her hands.

But only at,
her convenience.

Only at,
her craving.

Just to then
hide me away
and treat me so cold
when the rest of the house
awoke,
for a nice
warm breakfast.

Last Time

One day,
the complaining and nagging,
just stopped.

I assumed it was
because my efforts
were finally paying off.

All those late night
conversations
when we sat face to face,
and I gave her
my undivided attention
for her to be able to address
all of her concerns
and troubles.

I took notes,
both mentally
and physically.

I prayed on it.
I asked God for guidance
on how to help me
fix the things
she found to be so
wrong with me,
so that we could
move forward
and live,
happily ever after.

I assumed it all
stopped,
because of my efforts?

Instead,
she had only given me
the summary version
of what her issues
were with me.

What I was working on
to fix me,
were only a few
bullet points
off her long list of
"she's never going to change".

She kept the rest of the list
to herself,
and stored it deep inside her
where she knew,
I would never be able
to reach it.

She convinced herself
that the relationship was dead,
despite my dying desire
to try and save it.
She put me in her head
as a thing of the past,
while I was standing
right in front of her,
presently trying.

I thought,
the complaining and nagging
had stopped,
because we were finally on
the right path again.

But what it actually was,
was a mute warning,
that she was at the door,
putting her coat on
for the **last time.**

Wasted

To think,
she's replaced my touch
on her body
with another's hands.

My kiss
on her face
with another's lips.

My feelings
with another's heart.

My dreams
with another's soul.

It's only been
a couple of months,
and just like that,
our entire history is,
erased.

I see,
that like a snake,
she's shed all
that used to be us,
and has slithered her way
into a new hole
for nesting.

I feel bad
for the next victim
who gets to feel
her fangs,
and who is about to
slowly experience
the toxic poison within.
Oh, the amount of time
that's about to be,
wasted.

Skeletons

People will hurt you;
physically,
emotionally,
psychologically,
and more.

I don't even remember
how many times,
and in how many arguments
I had to tell her,
"I AM NOT THEM."

Yet there I was,
left standing on one side
of the battlefield,
that she created
and put me in.

Fighting against
ghost and demons
that only she
could see.

How was that
a fair battle?

I was destined to
lose that war
before I even stepped foot
in the field.

I hope the next partner
doesn't have to deal
with the same grenades
I had to deal with.

Ones that we're designed
to go off
right when she
needed them to.

How convenient.

Only she
had access
to the pins,
and she wore them
proudly around her fingers
like rings
of expensive taste.

I still wonder sometimes,
who was right
in that argument?
Her?
By saying it was
all my fault
that things ended?
Or me?
By saying we ended,
because she
just couldn't let go
of all her **skeletons?**

Mirage

Like thinking I see
water
in the desert,
I was tricked
into the hallucination
of her promises
about "forever".

Everything that ever
came from her lips,
was a real
optical phenomenon,
and I was the
vultures prey,
every time.

Glass House

Have you ever thought about
what it would look like,
if we could see into
each other's chest?

If everyone's hearts
were encased
in glass housing?

What if everyone had meters
attached to their hearts,
and we were able to see
how much pain
they carried in it,
the first day
we meet them?

What if we could see
how much love
they have left in it,
before we spend our nights
falling in love with them?

Would an experience
such as this,
be more happy,
or sad?

Would experiencing this,
be more helpful,
or counterproductive?

If people knew
how much pain
you were carrying around
with you everyday,

would they have treated you
better than they did?

I showed her my heart meter
from the very beginning,
and shared with her
the stories
of how I got there
and why my tank
was on empty.

She promised to be
the fuel
to fill me up
with a love
I've never experienced.

Instead,
I was taken
full advantage of.

All of my insecurities
that I entrusted her with,
she simply used
as matches
to gaslight me.

Her words were of heavy stones,
and she threw them at me
as hard as she could
on a daily basis.

So now,
I've made my heart
into a shallow hologram,
because of all the rocks
she threw,
at my **glass house.**

God Sent

I wasn't going anywhere.

Not out of her life
after any fight.

Not out for a drive
to sneak text another.

Not into the arms
of another woman
who bats her eyes at me.

I was here
to finally heal
her hurting.

I wonder how she's
taking the loss,
of leaving the one,
God sent?

Thirsty

She always had
a sweet tooth.

She admitted to being someone
always chasing after
the newest candy,
the newest flavors.

What she failed
to tell me,
was how she'd tend to
get parched
midway through
the honeymoon phase
at the beginning
of a new relationship.

How her thirst
was never quite
quenched,
no matter who
she was with.

She craved more than
what I could
supply her with.

I was boring old water,
which she gladly traded
for what she thought
was sweet tea.

Turns out
they were sour milk,
and she suddenly realized
just how nutritious I was
for our relationship.

The Storm

She wanted out of
the candy shop,
and back into
the healthy kitchen,
with me.

Well this kitchen is closed,
and this boring old water
has found a new glass
to pour herself in.

One who wants to hold
all of me,
take me in slow,
and taste me off
their lips
with eyes closed
and a smile on their face
because they know,
that we are,
healthy together.

How unfortunate,
that all these years later,
I hear she's still **thirsty,**
and searching for water.

Had Me Convinced

When I first looked
into her eyes,
I felt something.

It was a different feeling
I had never felt before.

Her smile was soft
and sweet,
and the promises
rolling off her lips
were even sweeter.

When she spoke,
my ADHD eased.
I focused.
I listened.

She had become
the only teacher
I wanted lessons by.

I loved her
the way I was
supposed to.

I treated her
with the utmost respect
and trust.

I thought she was
the angel on Earth
I had prayed for.

However, she wore
Hell Red
better than
Heaven White
and refused to fly
with me.

Instead she was
a heavy anchor,
keeping me from
the clouds.

At first,
I thought she was
my forever girl,
and now I feel
like a fool,
at how easily she
had me convinced.

Pity Her

When she said
"we need to talk",
I expected my heart
to sink,
into my stomach.

But how could it be
a bad thing,
when we just had
the most perfect date
all day yesterday?

Her ability to turn
her emotions
on and off like a
light switch
was never something
I envied.

Why would one choose
to only hold onto
the arguments and disagreements,
over all else,
even though the most
recent memory of
time spent together,
was so great?

It was almost like
she needed a fight
to feel secure.

The Storm

Because as soon as we
were good again,
she'd snap herself out of it
as if we couldn't just
stay there, and remain happy
in the clouds together.

We could never just move on either.
It was scarring,
and made me feel
scared for the happy moments when
they did happen to come around,
because I knew,
it wouldn't last long.

For this being the way
she chooses to live her life
"loving" others,
I **pity her.**

Past

At one point,
I could only see her
as my future.
But the present me
re-lives everything
she ever put me through,
and now I'm so glad
she's a part of
my **past.**

Trash

My level of hopeless romantic
is something I'm realizing
is not ever going to diminish.

My search for true love
will always outweigh
the reality of how many
red flags I see
or don't see
before me.

Most times,
in relationships like these,
I'm like a raccoon,
only seeing in
black and white
and who periodically catches
spots of gray
while rummaging for
something great,
through the dumpster.

All the while
forgetting that just because
I can't see the red flags,
doesn't make what I'm
searching through
any less
than what it is.
Trash.

Forgive, Than To Forget

She told me this
new girl,
didn't mean anything
to her.

But there was something
about this woman,
in that moment,
that made her better
than me.

In that moment,
I wasn't thought about
at all.

She didn't love me
that night.

Because if she had,
and if she did,
none of that
would have ever
happened.

Not then,
or the time after that,
or with the girl after her either.

Love doesn't run,
love doesn't hide,
and love doesn't lie
straight to the face it once
wanted to stand across the altar from
promising forever too.

She just kept lying,
over and over again

The Storm

like a record so broken
the song would've never
been heard the same again.

Her tongue was so sharp,
and yet the words rolling off of it
were so smooth.

And there I went,
forgiving her again
instead of listening
to my gut.

Instead of listening
to the screams
of my crying heart
demanding better of me.

She was never
going to change,
and I realized that the girl
I fell in love with,
was long gone.

Still, even knowing all of this
in those moments,
I kept all my feelings under
lock and key,
and cried myself to sleep
every night,
as quietly as I could
while she held me.

For some warped reason,
I didn't want to disturb her dreams
of these other women
while I laid in her arms.
But it was just so much easier
to **forgive, than to forget.**

Expectations

I expected her
to keep her promises,
because I kept mine.

I expected her
to be honest,
because I always was
with her.

I expected her
to never hurt me,
because never in a million years
would I have ever
hurt her.

I expected her
to not cheat on me,
and yet after every single
one of them,
I convinced myself to believe
that she was truly sorry.

Thanks to her,
I learned a lot about myself
in that relationship.

That I expect to be loved
the way I love others.

However,
I'm done trying to uphold
any **expectations**
from anyone moving forward,
because all it ever leads to
is disappointment.

Actually Loved Me

Love,
is when you speak highly of them,
even after a fight.

Love,
is when your words are soft and understanding,
even when you don't agree with the topic.

Love,
is when you behave like you're off the market,
because you are.

Love,
is when you dismiss the idea of competition amongst others,
because there isn't any.

Love,
is when your hands are strong with love and passion,
and not with anger and hate.

Love,
is when your present emotionally,
not just physically.

Love,
is when you ease insecurities,
not create more mind games.

Love,
is when you have their back
because you're a team
and that's your partner,
not throw them under the bus
for the popular vote or for the laugh.

Looking back,
I can see now
that she never
actually loved me.

Gamble

I always said
that I'm someone
who loves my money
too much to gamble,
and it's because I work
too hard to earn it,
just to lose it all
in the blink of an eye.

Yet, I gamble my heart
everyday that I choose
to give it to someone
who's already proven
can't be trusted with it.

My chances of winning
are slim to none,
but here I am
back again
to stick it in the slot,
eyes rolled,
toes crossed,
gasped breath,
in hopes that this time
I'll hit the jackpot with her.

Bust.

The game's over.

I lose again.

I keep winning nothing,
losing everything,
and here I am,
in the middle of the night,
at the same machine
in the same bed,
ready to **gamble.**

Too Late

I told her to stop
as her tricky lips
tried to fool me
one last time
on her way
out the door.

I wasn't needing
an apology,
no not anymore.

I learned to be able
to forgive her without it.
I learned to heal
despite her stubbornness
of throwing a fit.

She could never
admit fault,
and yet so much
she taught.

But I moved on,
dusting off the shelf,
ready to live,
happily with myself.

I experienced what it feels like
to never want her back.
It had finally clicked
as a matter of fact.

That there was no more us,
only me, and only her,
and I let her know
it's not **too late**
to forgive herself,
and to erase everything
that we ever were.

Season

I frequently have moments
of wondering,
if my destiny involves
never experiencing
a happily ever after?

People come and go
so frequently in my life,
that it sometimes feels
like I was put on this Earth
just to imprint on them.

Like I was just
supposed to have them
for a little while
and help them grow
into the person
they were destined to be.

To ready them
and prepare them
to find their true
soulmate.

The word that haunts me
the most these days
is "seasons".

However,
I'm not talking about
the weather.

Now don't get me wrong,
I absolutely love when
God chooses me
and uses me to be
one of his messengers,

or disciples through
these seasons,
and I'll never say otherwise.

It just sometimes feels like
in those low moments,
that I'm somebody who's
living a life in a body that has
a very long-term
heart and head in it,
but rather living
a very short-term reality.

Maybe once I realize
that I'm everyone's season
and not meant to stay forever,
that I will feel less pain,
less weight,
less anxiety,
less fear,
and less sorrow?

I am soon coming to
the realization
that those friends,
that fan,
that teacher,
that coach,
that girlfriend,
I may just be a **season** too,
and that I may not be meant
to stay in their lives forever.

So I guess this is like
the weather after all,
because these thoughts
and these emotions
feel like one hell of a storm.

DIRTY LAUNDRY & MEMORIES TO BURN

Pictures Of Her

My walls,
man are they empty.

My phone,
light from all the pictures
and videos removed.

I can't bare it,
the thought of looking at
them anymore.

The memories that come
flooding in,
the emotions that come
rushing back.

My eyes,
man are they blurry.

From the fullness of water
being held back in them.

So I close them slowly,
and let the tears
fall effortlessly.

The longer they're closed
the wetter my cheeks.

My chest hurts.

With bowed head,
I can see them all
like flash cards
flipping through my brain.

Every image as clear
as the sun filled day we took it.

This hurts,
and I just want the pain,
to stop.

So I force my eyes open
to bring myself
back to reality.

Just to then
be reminded again,
by the bare walls
that used to hold
the **pictures of her.**

In Love With Her

She was texting me
while she was still,
with her.

Something wasn't
adding up.

She was still
holding her hand
instead of mine,
and it let me know
that she wasn't
disliking her current position
as much as she was
leading me on to believe
she was.

She insisted on telling me
in every conversation we had,
that she still loved me.
I still loved her too.
I wasn't allowed to say it
out loud though.
Cause that made her feel bad.

She insisted on telling me
in every conversation we had,
that she was trying to
figure it all out.
Figure out if she was
in love with her
the same way she was
in love with me.

It made me question
why she was still talking to
me then?

If this new girl
hasn't done anything wrong,
and she's everything
that has ever been prayed for,
then why am I
still responding
like a love drunk idiot
to her 3:00 a.m. text?

I always wondered if
the new girl got butterflies,
the way I still did?

I always wondered if
the new girl craved her touch,
like I still did?

You see,
when you're in love
with someone,
truly in love with them,
there's never a shadow of a doubt
in your mind about them.

Every fiber
of your being,
every beat
in your heart,
and every feeling
in your soul,
tingles with excitement
and confidence,
because it knows,
"that's my girl."

The Storm

If I ever had to think about
whether or not
she was my soulmate,
she wouldn't be.

This new girl had swooped in,
and she loved it,
the attention,
the gifts,
the sweet nothings.

But you see,
you can't confuse
kindness and friendship,
with love.

For a while,
only I could see
that this friendship of theirs
had cracks in it,
and it was only me
that knew in my heart and soul
that she was not really,
in love with her.

Her Things

I almost broke
my ankle,
trying to grab
my phone.

Warped excitement
filled my bones.

All it mentioned was
about when she could
come to get her things.

Poison filled the air
surrounding my beautiful cloud
of butterflies that were
residing in my belly.

Dead.
Mirroring the image of how
I then felt inside.

The silence that followed
was almost unbearable.

For that to have been
the only topic
of discussion
between us now
was absolutely,
gut-wrenching.

If I'm being honest
with myself,
I felt pathetic.

The Storm

Pathetic for having wanted
those conversations
to happen anyway,
because it was better than silence
or nothing at all.

After all,
she did leave me
in the middle of the night
and gave me no chance
to tell her
how I really felt.

To tell her
how much I actually
loved her.

She had jammed
as many of her
clothes into trash bags
as she could,
and the dog was happy
to be joining her
like they were going on
some kind of spontaneous
road trip.

But I had to work,
and so there was
no stopping
this action by her.

I'll be honest,
I thought she
was bluffing.

Now,
I'm sorry that
she wasn't.

I assumed she was
out for a night drive
to clear her head,
so she could come
back home to me,
fresh mind and
ready to talk so we could
resolve whatever it was
that was sitting heavy
on her heart.

As I reminisced
on all of this hurt,
the only thing I could think
to text back was,
"hey babe".

And then I waited.

I waited for what seemed
to feel like decades
for the reply text that she
was sorry and coming home.

But that text never came,
and so I thought to myself,
'this is it,
and I wonder when
she's coming
to get the rest of
her things.'

Ultimatum

I can't remember
exactly how long
it took me
to finally realize
that if she wanted this again,
she would be here.

She would have already
come back by now.

She wasn't going to leave
where she was currently planted,
which was in the arms
of someone new.

I also don't know
if it would hurt any less
if she would've met this girl
after we ended.

Instead of it being the girl
that she hid from me
while we were still
in a relationship?

I knew she hated ultimatums,
but there came a time
where a choice
needed to be made.

I was still in love
and blinded myself
with how bright my heart
shinned for her.

But I also knew
that I didn't deserve
this level of
misleading behavior
as much as
the new girl didn't.

I laid all of my cards
on the table,
one last time,
with my front door and arms
wide open for her,
and she chose to
slam the door shut
with the answer she was
never brave enough
to give me to my face.

She was going to stay
with her,
no matter what was said that day.

One of the last things
she ever texted me,
was that she loved me
and always would.

Then mentioned that if we
were ever single
at the same time,
that I should "hit a girl up".

The Storm

Out of everything that we
had talked about that evening,
she managed to do
what she did best,
and turn the tables
pointing the finger at me
yet again.

And like a magician
performing her final trick,
by the end of our conversation,
I ended up being the one
with the **ultimatum.**

Could Sleep

I had come first,
but she was 'the now'.

Thoughts of their
newly found happiness
made me stir at night.

I should've just moved on,
but I decided to check my phone
that night instead.

It was a never-ending war
between my head and my heart
on such a topic.
Missing her.

How dare I keep doing this
to myself.

After all,
I told her to, right?
To leave?

I said it
out of pure frustration.
And for once,
she listened to me.

So why can't I
ever listen to me?

Advice better given
than received by self I guess?

I remember the night we were texting
and her new lover repositioned
to the other shoulder
to hold her.

I told her
to put her phone down
so that her lover didn't see
the 3:00 a.m. glow
of our pictures
on her face.

I had wondered if
the lover's subconscious
knew about us?

Because she started holding her
closer and tighter,
as if she didn't want to lose her
the way I just had.

The lover didn't want her
to fall out of love,
like she had just
fallen out of love with me.

I wondered how
the lover would have felt
knowing that I was
still the one
being talked to and missed
at 3:00 a.m.
every night?

How "coming home" and
"being a family again"
was a daily topic
of our conversations.

Spooning was one of her favorite
sleeping positions, after all,
and it had crossed my mind
a time or two
if the lover had felt to her
as good as I did?

If the lover made her feel
as safe,
as I always did?

Well I guess not
if she decided to always text me
while the lover slumbered
next to her obliviously.

Our time for that night
was cut short,
and we were both left awake,
staring at the wall,
and neither of us,
could sleep.

Third Heart

She said
someone else's heart
was involved now.

She said
it was because
the one she truly wanted,
me,
had instructed her to move on.

Well yes,
I did do that,
but of course,
I didn't mean it.

I hate when
emotions in moments,
take over and speak
before it's been
proofread first.

She knew every
button to push,
and she waited until
I had enough,
so that she could use that
and run away with it.

There were typos and errors
in the words I spoke that day,
but I see now
she never really wanted me
to edit and resubmit.

She was so quick to tell me
that it was too late
and that she was never
going to leave her,
even though I knew
they started their relationship
way before her and I,
ever ended.

It was in that moment
that I realized
the match was over,
and the **third heart**
had won.

Misled

Every time she spoke
as soft as the clouds,
I'd be roped back in.

I would feel like
we were finally
on the same page again.

It felt like my girl
was coming home,
but for real this time.

Until she said
she needed to discuss it over
with "her"
and then canceled the trip
to come see me.

If someone wanted
to be with me,
what would they need
to discuss
and with who?

Every time she spoke
like knives lived on her tongue,
I just wanted to disappear.

I hated going in circles,
and I hated that in
every other conversation,
I was being told that
I was not,
the choice she chose.

In one moment,
I was told that I wasn't
good enough,
and then the very next moment,
I was told she wanted me
to hold her.

In one moment,
I was told that I was
never going to change,
and then the very next moment,
I was told my kisses were
being deeply missed
on her lips.

The company I kept
while waiting on an answer
from her,
warned me about this thing
called karma.

And I guess this is exactly
what they meant,
by feeling **misled.**

Got Away

There were often moments
that I sat in the
silence of the night
and just thought.

Sometimes I thought about
how I almost wished
she had done me dirty.

Said something,
did something,
anything.

Just so I had an excuse
and a reason
to tell myself
why she was no good for me.

To remind myself
that she's in fact
not the one.

But there was nothing.

Nothing but the mind-blowing
memories we had made together.

Nothing but the fun times.
Nothing but the love
we shared.

I wondered about how
the kids were doing,
and then I'd have to
snap myself out of it.

I wondered how our
stubborn little puppy was doing,
and then I'd have to
slap myself back to reality.

At first when she left
I wanted to hear about
all the new hiking spots
she had to have found by now,
ones that we would never
get to experience together
but still somehow felt
tied to knowing about.

I couldn't get her
out of my mind
and I just wanted
someone to tell me
how to get the thoughts
and feelings, under control.

I couldn't reach out and ask her
because I knew she was going
through the same pain,
at least I hoped that she was.

I hoped this was as hard for her,
as it was for me.

That if 'we' had ever really
meant anything to her at all,
she'd be feeling this too.

The Storm

I got through it by
creating stories
that were a little less sad
to tell myself,
just to temporarily mask
the thoughts of heartache
and misery of what
actually happened.

Looking back on it,
I have learned to relive the memories
for exactly what they were
and for the way
that they happened.

I know now that she was
removed from my life
for the most healthy of reasons,
and I thank God everyday
for letting her be the one
that **got away.**

Map

Everyday I stare
at the near empty map
that's hanging on my wall.

The one I bought for us
and our travel memories.

Our hikes,
and newly found cafes
to sip coffee at
in the sunlight through the
store's windows.

Our favorite restaurants
and recently discovered friends,
from all across the globe.

It was for our dog park
memories in all 50 states
that we got to take
our babies to.

But we only saw
a handful together
before realizing I guess,
that I wasn't her
forever travel partner.

Now there's someone new
taking her pictures
at the edge of
every cliff.

The Storm

There's someone new
who gets to kiss her
at the bottom of
every waterfall.

And everyday,
I sit here
alone with the dogs
drinking coffee by myself
in the warmth of the
sunlight through my
own homes windows,
and I get to stare
at the near empty **map**,
that's hanging on my wall.

Guilty

I feel bad for
loving her.

She made me feel
like I wasted
10 months of each
of our lives.

Like I was some kind of
horrible criminal
that broke in
and stole her heart away
from the more worthy,
then I was.

She just didn't know
how it felt to actually
be loved
for who she was
with no conditions.

She didn't know
what to do with it
when she had it,
and so instead of just
embracing it,
she made me feel **guilty**
for ever loving her.

Complacent

I realize it now,
looking back.
I can see it
as clear as day.

She was gone
long before
she actually left.

You see,
I thought she left that night.

The night I had to
go to work,
and she said that if I left,
she would see it,
as abandonment.

When she said it
out loud,
there was a
familiarity to it.

Where had I heard this story
about abandonment before?

I kicked myself
for days on end
about not just
calling out that night
and staying home
with her instead.

I blamed myself for
being the reason
she left.

For being a responsible adult
and going to work
as I was supposed to.

But had I called out that night,
and had I not gone to
work and chosen to stay home
with her instead,
the outcome would have
been the same.

Except, in addition
to losing her,
I may have also
lost my career.

It had finally clicked,
and then I remembered
where I had heard
that story before.

She had told me
that her ex-wife left her,
in the middle of the night,
with no warning,
and how she wasn't there
to be able to save
her marriage.

It's funny how patterns
seem to work in life.

I was so good to her,
physically and emotionally,
yet all she ever wanted to do
was pick a fight.

The Storm

It was beyond sad,
but it was because
that's what she was so used to
from her previous partners.
That's the only way she has
ever been 'loved' by anyone close
to her before me.

It was unimaginable,
and I couldn't blame her.

She couldn't handle the realization
of finally being loved genuinely,
not just by me,
but by my entire family.

It saddened me
for our future
knowing she was too far gone
to save.

It's incredibly unfortunate
that I didn't have wider eyes
from the beginning.

She stopped talking to someone
so she could start talking to me.

I should've known better.

Inevitably, that's also
how we ended.

Same toxic pattern,
different day,
different chick.

Now there's a new relationship
with the girl she was talking to
behind my back,
and it's because she's stuck
in the only pattern she knows
how to live in.

The pattern of thinking
that life is always greener
on the other side,
now has her in a position
of ruining this new girl's life too.

It's really a shame,
especially because the new girl
has no idea
how uninterested in her
she really is.

I loved her once,
and still believe that she
deserves true happiness,
and so I just pray that one day
she wakes up,
and learns how to stop living
such a temporarily
complacent
lifestyle.

Home Wrecker

She said
she was unhappy
with the new situation
and regretted,
leaving me.

Every single day
she told me
she missed me,
and that she was still very much
in love with me.

We got into detail
during our late night conversations
while she slept
next to someone new,
about how she was
going to find her way
back to me.

How she was going to
fix the mistakes
made in the past
so that this time around
we would be a success story.

Until it was time to put actions
to those words,
in which she failed me
every time.

Nothing but more misleading
empty promises
that left me in a limbo status
of waiting on her next move.

But waiting on her
to take charge of a situation
and make a move
in my direction,
was like playing chess
by myself.

I'm the only one who
was ever brave enough
to make a move,
and I had to do so
for both sides,
all the time.

She must have gotten cold feet
because she froze
and didn't move an inch towards me
when she said she wanted to.

How does one become
so good at manipulating
two different minds
at the same time?

Having us both believing
that we were who she was
the most in love with?

That we were
more important,
than the other chick?

That we were
who she actually wanted
to marry
and spend the rest
of her life with?

The Storm

We're both idiots,
and we both deserve
so much better
than someone like her.

The difference between
my competition and I
is that I actually know
who the real version
of her is now.

I know the truth
behind her eyes,
and the evil
that resides within.

I've seen first hand
and experienced
how manipulating
she can actually be.

Eventually, she'll hurt this girl too,
but I, thankfully,
made it out,
and I did not let her back in.

I truly feel now that they
should have each other.

After all,
my competition fought so hard
to slip in between us
and steal her away from me
in the first place,
so the least she could do,
is just stay with her.

Lindsey Kay Atkinson

I suppose they
deserve each other,
and I sure do hope they enjoy
this new life of theirs,
with their own
little personal **home wrecker.**

Hope She's Happy

I wonder if they
know about us
now that it's over?

Her mother?
The one who was so sad
to see her leave
and move to my state with me.
Well she's back home now.
I hope she's happy.

Does she know about us?
Her sister?
The one she'd always call
when we would disagree about something.
The one who always told her to leave me
instead of talking things out?
I hope she's happy.

Does she know about us?
Her new best friend?
The girl who was my ex before her,
that at one point in life
we despised together?
Knowing them,
they probably think
they have the last laugh?
I hope she's happy.

Does she know about us?
Her daughter?
The one who asked us
to get married.
The one who wanted me
to be her stepmom and who always
hoped we'd be together forever?

The little girl who she promised
to keep me in her life always?
I hope she's happy.

Does she know about us?
Her girlfriend?
The one who she waits for
to fall asleep
so that she can sneak text me
at 3:00 a.m.,
telling me how much
she misses me
and how in love with me
she still is?

The girlfriend she contemplated leaving
for months
while dragging my heart
along every thorn she could find,
up the empty promise stem,
to the beautiful rose of
"I'm coming home".

Well, I've recently taken those
rose colored glasses off,
and I wonder if she knows,
she's laying next to
a beautiful liar
every night?

Oh well,
not my problem anymore,
and I sure **hope
she's happy.**

Quid Pro Quo

I showed her my heart again,
not because I wanted
something from her,
but because I was still
in love with her.

She told me sweet nothings
everyday,
and she did it so well,
that I actually believed her,
again.

She roped me back in
and I flirted.

I talked with her everyday
after our split,
and we yet again,
started making
future plans together.

I would tell her
every single night
how in love with her
I still was,
before she went to bed.

Unbeknownst to me,
as I was doing so,
she was quietly climbing into bed
with another,
who was telling her the same.

Had I known
that this engagement with her
would just be another mind game
of **quid pro quo**,
and that the word 'engagement'
had already belonged
to the other woman
only four months later,
I would have saved my heart the trouble,
and just stayed gone
for good.

Necklace

We argued
over that stupid necklace
for damn near
6 months.

She was the first,
and the only human being
who could not only convince me
that putting all of my
walls down for her
would be a good idea,
but then who also
successfully accomplished it.

A near impossible task,
she achieved effortlessly
with the blink of an eye.

No longer did
trust issues,
insecurities,
or jealousy
have control
over my life.

Not anymore,
thanks to her and the love
she had to give me.

I felt like for the first time
in my life,
she had cured me.

Like she was
some kind of love guru
who had come along
and finally healed all of my years
of betrayal and hurt.

In my head and
in my heart,
it was her and I
against the world.

But then one night
while laying next to me in bed,
when we could have easily
been holding each other
and loving one another,
she decided to spend that time
on her phone instead.

She stayed on it,
until it literally died.

She then turned to face me
on the bed,
and even though slightly
annoyed with her,
I was finally happy to have
my girl
all to myself.

But that's not what
ended up happening.

No, she instead asked
ever so politely
if she could use my phone.

The Storm

Her phone dying
wasn't received as a sign
from God
to get off of it,
and to spend quality time
with her loyal girlfriend
who was patiently waiting
and laying right next to her,
craving for her attention.

No.
Texting her "friend"
was more important
at the time.

At least that's what she
had convinced me of.

A couple weeks later
someone sent her a package
to the house.

To my house.

Full of goodies,
"I'm thinking about you's"
and more.

Again,
convinced that this was
"just a friend",
I decided to bite my tongue,
and stayed quiet.

In that package,
was also a necklace.

One in which she immediately
replaced the necklace
I had given her.

We argued
over that stupid necklace
for damn near
6 months.

Fast forward to only
5 months after she left me,
and imagine
the brilliant work of God
right as I started to let her
slip back into my heart,
as He exposed her
for who she truly is.

I was minding my own business
at my parents house,
spending quality time
with my family
and trying to keep myself
distracted from all the hurting
and the heartbreak that
I was experiencing
because of her.

When in pops a Snap suggestion
based off of my phone's
'saved contacts.'

Well what do you know,
it's her "friend".
The friend with no name.

The Storm

She must have saved their number
in my phone that day,
because on this day,
all of the pieces finally fit together
and this friend
now had a name,
and a face.

Less than a month after that,
this "friend" had become
her fiancé.

And now,
it all made sense,
as to why we argued
over that stupid **necklace**
for damn near
6 months.

Prisoner

Her hand on my throat
was only welcomed
sometimes.

When it was passion-filled,
it was hot.

But other times,
I would feel her
squeezing tightly
against my trachea
in a manner of
silence.

It was almost as if
she was trying to
imprison the words
from escaping my lips.

The words of doubt,
trust issues,
and insecurities.

If I didn't speak about them,
they didn't exist.

If I didn't mention it,
then we were alright.
Right?

Every word I ever said,
got pitched to her
straight over the mound
while she stood there,
stance ready,
bat up,
and ready to swing in defense

and use everything I ever said
against me, like a weapon.
I might as well have just
handed her the ammo.

All of her insecurities
I needed to hush
and reassure daily,
and yet with mine,
she made sure to put them
under a magnifying glass
for all the world to see,
and then said it was
my fault
for even feeling those ways.

She made me feel bad
for ever having them
in the first place.

These insecurities
and trust issues
that were now
embedded in me.

Issues that I had no control over,
she made sure to add fuel to,
instead of keeping her promises
of loving me through them,
the way I loved her through hers.

Throughout that entire relationship,
I always viewed her
as my partner.

But to her,
I see now that I was never
anything more,
than her **prisoner.**

Screaming Match

There were nights
I couldn't get a word in.

There were nights
that she couldn't either.

We shared many
unpleasant moments together,
especially towards the end,
where it became unbearable
to even try being
in the same room
as each other.

Why did it last so long?

Why didn't we just
let go sooner?

Was that us
actually fighting
to save it?

Or were we both
already checked out?

Too far gone
and sucked into the
drama warp
of our new normal?

Fighting with one another
became our
drug of choice.

The Storm

We chose to get
higher and higher
even over the others
cries of surrender.
Why couldn't we
just stop?

What was so addicting
about staying
and belittling the other?

Why did we continue
time and time again
to prolong a pain
that could have easily been
avoided all together?

Well she's been gone for
quite a while now,
yet here I am,
still losing to screaming matches.

Who would have thought
I would lose a
screaming match,
to my own
crying echoes.

Record Of Wrong

I gave her the
absolute world.

She was essentially
my first,
and in a way,
who I truly came out for.

I was young,
dumb,
and in love.

But I'm sure you've read
this book before.

The one where
'one lesbian meets another
and they fall in love.'

She was older,
seemed wiser,
more experienced,
and had many more
adult relationships
under her belt
than I'd ever had.

Yet, something about the
young mature me,
sparked a flame in her
that the others she had prior,
never could.

I watched as our relationship
Blossomed.

The Storm

The student,
becoming the teacher.

I taught her things,
and surprised her
with my level of love
and commitment
at such a young age.

She would think out loud
about how this could be so good
for my first lesbian relationship,
when she had
been through so many
that were not even remotely
close to this.

Well, instead of
taking it all in,
and keeping it to
herself forever,
she took it all for granted,
and ripped my heart
straight out of
my chest.

I gave her the
trust and freedom
to do what she wanted
without being
a neck breather.

I was fresh and untouched
to the feelings of
hurt,
to pain,
and to heartbreak.

She interpreted that freedom
as utilizing her free will,
in unloving ways to my heart.

The fingers were always
pointed at me,
like I'm who forced her
to do those terrible things.

There wasn't anyone
threatening her or daring her
to make these decisions
of betrayal towards me.

She did everything
on her own.

And these other people,
they would simply
reach out to her,
and ask if they could give her
the attention
she was so willing to
receive by them,
and she'd confirm.

Always craving attention
from someone else.

Then they'd get what
they came for,
and throw her to the side
to come crawling
back to me.

And I was always there,
to pick her up
where she fell.

The Storm

I've learned over the years
to not keep a
record of wrong,
but the one thing
I can't forget
no matter how
hard I try,
is that she is
single-handedly
the originator,
of the trust issues
and insecurities
that I'm still battling
with today.

Fooled

After a decade
of building up walls
and closing myself off
to those who wanted
a chance with me,
she popped in
out of nowhere
and with the bat of an eye,
melted my heart
and calmed my soul.

I was so thrown off by this
unexpected reaction to her,
that I didn't for a second
question it.

She made me feel ways
I had only dreamed about.

I prayed for her,
for years,
and then out of the blue,
there she was.

I had put her
on a pedestal,
above every other human
I had ever been with,
and within weeks,
I knew I wanted to
make her mine forever.

She pretended to
want the same,
and became the
perfect liar.

Oh,
how she **fooled** me.

Exhausting

I got burned
pretty bad
trying to keep our
fire alive.

Yet instead of
walking away from something
so painful that continued
to hurt me,
I would just glove up
and try again.

Every day for her
was like gloving up
to fight,
and all I was trying to do
was layer myself
with protection
to keep trying.

She never saw it
as me trying,
and I couldn't help her
with that.

I hope her next relationship
doesn't have to gear up
just to love her
like I had to,
because honestly
it's heavy,
and absolutely
exhausting.

I Knew This

The fact that she wouldn't
let them go,
was a red flag for me.

But she had convinced me
that it 'shouldn't be red'.

The fact that she could have
let them go,
but refused to do so
because of the
'history between' them,
made chills
run up my spine.

The fact that we had
countless conversations
about how and why
this bothered me,
should've been my
wake up call.

And yet,
in the very moment of
discussing it again,
she blew me off
to take a phone call
from that person
in that exact moment.

That should've been
the final straw.

Right then and there
was my que to exit.
Of course, I didn't.

The Storm

But I guess the spells
she had put me under,
weren't scheduled to wear off
until after,
she left me for her.

The reality of the situation
was that she was still
in love with her ex.

I knew this,
I saw this,
and yet,
I stayed anyway.

Pieces

She came out of nowhere,
and returned the heart
that I thought,
was buried forever.

This heart,
it was bruised,
beaten,
and then shattered,
into a hundred pieces,
and hidden deep
into multiple graves,
scattered all over the country
where it had been
broken at.

This girl in particular,
she loved me.

Like no one had ever
loved me before,
and she proved it.

She did this
by going to each grave site
while I slept,
and retrieved each piece
of this broken heart,
on her own time.

She did this,
because she loved me.

The Storm

Everyday for her was
a new journey,
to find a new piece,
buried deep within
my broken past.

She learned every story
behind every break.

She put the work in.

She worked hard
behind scenes,
learning every weakness of mine,
every flaw,
and every ounce of pain,
that I was ever caused.

She made sure to
promise me daily
that she'd never
add to that pain.

She also reassured me daily
that God himself
had sent her to me,
to heal all of this pain,
once and for all.

She spent countless months
gathering the broken pieces
of my heart,
and then was brave enough
to confront me

with asking about the stories
and the people behind those stories
of who broke it,
and why.

So I opened up,
and I vulnerably told her,
everything.

She didn't have to ask,
but she loved me.

She said she wanted to
heal me,
and that in order to do so,
she needed to
understand everything,
from every angle.

I believed every word
she ever told me,
as if I hadn't been
lied to and burned
by others in the past.

Like I hadn't been
taking advantage of,
and my vulnerabilities
used against me
creating more weaknesses.

No,
not with her.

I trusted her with
everything in me.

The Storm

We sat side by side,
speaking into
each other's souls
while putting the pieces
back together,
and waiting for the
glue of promises
and healing,
to dry it.

I had never felt
that good
in my entire life,
and I couldn't believe
that my heart
was finally about to be
whole again.

This beautiful heart
that resided in my chest
for the longest time
broken and shattered,
was finally fixed,
and it was all because,
she loved me.

Whole, and complete again,
I saw it,
my heart,
sitting fragile in the palms
of her hands.

As I reached out lovingly
to retrieve it,
with the biggest smile
on my face,
that's when I realized
the blank stare on hers.

Who was this girl,
as I had never seen her before.

She looked different
from the one
I fell in love with
all of a sudden.
Eyes cold, and dark.

She intensely kept
eye contact with me,
as I saw in slow motion
her hands,
beginning to part.

She knew exactly
what she was doing,
and what it would do to me
if she let go,
but she did it anyway.

Her hands separated
as I watched
the last several months
of hard work,
love,
and promises,
become gravity's best friend.

It was as though I was
in slow motion.

I couldn't catch it.

It shattered,
right before my eyes,
and she waited
and watched

with a subtle smirk,
to witness the introduction
between tear and cheek
on my face.

Then she simply
turned around,
and walked away.

I never saw her again
after that.

I told her what hurt me the most,
and she did it perfectly.

She did it because,
she did not love me.

With bowed head
and scarred soul,
I slumped to the closet
to retrieve the broom,
and began sweeping up
the **pieces**,
yet again.

Shadows

It's crazy to me
how she truly believed
I'd never find out
about them.

She played it so well.

Both sides
defending her side
and she was actually able
to pin us
against each other.

How one's mind
could physically work that way,
be that manipulating,
and successfully get
two people
from two different walks of life
falling in love with her
at the same time,
is beyond me.

I felt so stupid.

They probably did too.

And yet she
felt nothing at all,
for either of our pain.

No regret,
no sympathy,
no apology.

The Storm

None of this phased her
because the reality is,
neither of us
actually meant
anything to her.

We were her pawns,
and the stepping stones
for her next adventure.

That's why she
drug us both along
for as long as she did,
and for as far as she had.

The only difference,
is I have self-love
and a higher moral standard
for myself than they did.

They stayed with her,
and truly believed
they had won.

I'm sorry but,
that's not a prize I'd ever
want to win.

I hope they both enjoy
the feeling of this
temporarily sweet victory,
and get a cavity.

She's someone that needs to have
her cake and eat it too,
but once it's consumed,
there's no regurgitation.

It's gone forever,
and on to the next bakery
she'll be.

Like the snake she is,
this new one will be
gone soon too,
in the next swallow,
once her sweet tooth
emerges from the
shadows again.

One-Way

I'm crazy.
I'm over dramatic.
I'm different.
I'm strange.
I'm too goofy.
I'm loud.
I'm obnoxious,
and I'm cocky.

These were some of her
description words
to me,
about me.

Mine for her were;
Beautiful.
Smart.
Godly.
Selfless.
Dreamy.
Motherly.
Sexy.
Patient,
and kind.

When I say them out loud
back to back like that,
I see what my loved ones
were talking about now.

I see what they saw
as a fly on the wall
listening in on her
demeaning conversations to me,
and how she always
tried to crush my spirits
whenever possible.

All while I'm talking her up
and giving her the
unconditional love
I promised her I would.

Like a beat dog,
I would always limp back to
my abuser
in hopes that this time,
she'd love me back.

The reality of our
love story however,
was me constantly
running circles around her
on her private little
one-way street.

Ruined Us

I think for the duration
of our relationship,
she had this false
idea of me.

I think she expected me
to be that visually perfect,
always happy
and always funny person
that she fell in love with
at the club that night.

I wonder if she only
fell harder for me
because so many other fish
were biting?

I ignored all that,
and I had chosen her,
not for her looks,
the amount of attention
others were wanting
to give to her,
or because of the
amount of money
she brought with her
that evening.

No, I saw
true potential,
and she made me
feel hopeful,
for a future again.

It's unfortunate that material
is all that she'll
ever see.

She'll only ever see
dollar signs
instead of seeing
the way someone
wants to treat her heart.

She'll only ever see
fake lashes,
nails,
and hair extensions,
instead of envisioning
a future with someone.

I think she pretends to be
hard and tough,
when in reality all she truly wants
is soft hands,
holding her heart
and treating her soul right.

Until she has that anyway,
and then it's no longer
of interest to her.

She takes those
soft loving hands
and cuts them up
with razor blades
out of mythical defense
from the skeletons
in her past.

The Storm

Skeletons that she blames
on whoever she's with,
and then wonders why it is
that people never want
to try to reach for her again.

I think she had this false idea of me,
and looking back I see now,
that it's what **ruined us.**

Bully

She held me
like no other ever had.

She gave me hope,
brought me joy,
made me happy,
just to take it all away
because she could.

She was like the bully
from high school
who would call me gay
making everyone else
laugh at me,
just to then pick me to be
on her dodgeball team.

With a snap of a finger
she would have my emotions flip
from despising her one moment,
to then somehow being grateful
and feeling lucky,
for being able to even
be apart of her life
the very next.

And like the bully
to throw the ball
at the back of their own
teammates head
for one last laugh,
she waited to break up with me
in public
so all of her friends
could attend such a showing.

The Storm

Myself, casted as the
lead character
playing the role of
embarrassment.

I had spent hours that night
getting ready to come out
and meet up with her.

I made sure to
look my best,
and made sure to
smell of her favorite
cologne of mine.

I just wanted to impress her,
and make her happy.

I was in route
with my head held high
ready to take on the night.

The worst part about it was,
that she told me to come out
because she wanted
to have a date night.

A one-on-one,
so we could move past
our differences
and look forward
to the future.

What I actually walked into,
was her new girlfriend
lurking in the shadows
of the corner of the bar,
with some of their friends

for a front row seat
to the heartbreak misery,
I was invited into that evening.
After being the laugh of their party,
I got to cry a long 45 minute
drive home,
alone,
heartbroken,
while she stayed
to make out with her new lover
and dance all their worries away.

She knew what she did
and how she had done it
was wrong.

She didn't care.

Not as long as the crowd
was laughing at anyone,
but her.

I guess she forgot
what it felt like
to be laughed at,
or the fact that she had
shared all of those stories with me
from her bullied past.

Crazy to think
that the once bullied,
has now become
the ultimate **bully.**

Closed Doors

I had witnessed
the way she loved,
before I knew her.

It was beautiful,
and I prayed to
experience a love
like that myself
one day.

Then as time passed
and stars aligned,
I got to experience
that love firsthand.

It was even more beautiful,
once it was mine.

Now, I'm a ghost
of her past
because the way she loved
was based on
too many conditions.

I can only hope that
her next person
doesn't get their hopes up
like I did.

Thinking they're getting into
the most loving relationship,
just to realize
it's the complete opposite
behind **closed doors.**

Publicity

I wondered how long
it would last?

A city girl from New York
who takes the subway
everywhere she goes,
with her two Chihuahuas
in a hand bag.

Then me,
a southern heart,
needing the radio blasting
with all the windows down
for the German Shepherds
in the back seat.

An unlikely pair,
finding love at the most
unlikely time.

I wonder why we actually
got together anyway?

Possibly the excitement of her
getting to date a well known,
well liked,
popular lesbian YouTuber?

Or maybe,
the excitement of me
getting to finally attend
a NYC pride?

The Storm

We made a duet
on my channel,
because I wanted
her singing voice
to be known
to the world.

I took a greyhound
back and forth
from suburb to city
every few weeks,
building a bond and
sharing cultural differences
so effortlessly with her.

The day she met
my grandparents,
and the day I
watched her dad
perform theater with her,
those were important
days to me,
and yet
meant nothing to her.

When I'm with
someone I love,
I have a horrible habit of
pushing others away
who are close to me.

I lost one of the
most important people
in my life at the time,
because of this girl.

She made it seem
worth it,
and said it was her and I,
forever.

She told me that I had
no other option
but to let this friend go,
at least,
if I wanted to remain in a relationship
with her.

Once I did,
she completely changed,
for the worst.

She invited someone to
lunch with us,
someone new she had
never mentioned to me before.

This person,
they kept their distance
from me.

She then invited that person
to pride with us,
and again, I noticed how she
kept her distance from me.

It wasn't until the
subway ride home,
when I caught her dramatic
eye roll and scoff
at the mere site of me
holding the hand
of my girlfriend.

The Storm

I knew right then and there
that this person
was someone different to her
then what she had introduced them
to me as.

But the real red flag
was the night of the party.

She made a scene,
and left the party early
because she 'couldn't stand
seeing us happy together.'

How strange
for a 'friend'
to act that way.

How awkward,
knowing that her and I had
taken pictures together
the night of that party.

Any friend of my girl,
I wanted to be a friend
of mine.

I can only imagine
what she was thinking
as the lens closed us in
the same frame together.

Her, knowing what the two of them
actually had,
going on behind my back.

Her, knowing the truth of
the other side
of those text conversations,
with me just on the other side
of the room observing it.

Observing the looks being shot
from one to the other,
all night long,
each trying to stay composed
and not exposed.

I watched her slowly turn
my girlfriend against me,
and into a monster.

The kind of monster who
breaks up with someone
via phone call,
on their anniversary
while they're at work,
and then completely
ghost them forever.

When I found out
that the songwriter
was who she left me for,
it all started to make sense.

So thank you anyway,
but next.

I guess after all this time
that has passed,
I actually appreciate her
for leaving when she did.

The Storm

Because I'm chasing
after love,
and all she'll ever chase
is the next level
of **publicity.**

Hike

You should have seen her
while she hiked.

I trailed behind her
and watched,
observing her like an
undiscovered model.

The sun kissing off her tan
glowing skin.

I could have cried
at the memory
of how beautiful she was,
when she was encapsulated
by Jesus's creations
surrounding her.

She breathed the air,
differently.

She observed his creatures,
differently.

She appreciated his creation
in the mountains
and in the trees
and in all things his.

You should have seen her
when she was done.

The Storm

When she had reached the top
of the trail,
mountain,
or waterfall
she was so eager
to get to.

She was a daredevil.

And must sit with her legs
dangling off each cliff,
as if it were
solely the trophy
she was anticipating
to win.

She would smile,
but not with teeth.

It was the deepest
most beautiful grin
that you'd ever witness.

She had dimples
as deep as the
Grand Canyon
to accent it.

She would rest back
on her hands,
unscathed by the rocks
digging into her palms.

That kind of pain
never phased her.

She would tilt her head back
with eyes closed,
and let every sunbeam
kiss her face.

Her long beautiful
blonde hair
would hang effortlessly
straight off her head,
as if it were looking straight up
into the sky,
with her.

She would whisper softly,
"I love you",
and even though I was
there with her,
I wouldn't say it back.

I knew in these moments,
something special
was happening.

Instead I smiled,
and I watched her.

I was so happy knowing that
in THAT moment,
the 'I love you' rolling off of her lips
was in fact directed
to mother nature,
and to God.

After all,
this is where she said
she felt Him
the strongest,
the deepest.

The Storm

In those moments with her,
it was all I ever wanted,
and all I had ever
prayed for,
to marry one day.

Too bad I was seen
as unworthy,
and someone new
is wearing the ring
that was once
promised to me,
on that **hike.**

Villain

If she was so unhappy,
why didn't she just leave?

Why wouldn't she have just
ended things between us?

It was because she
needed me,
to be the bad guy.

She needed me,
to be the one to
close the book.

She needed someone
other than herself,
to take responsibility for
the relationship ending,
and so she stayed.

Stayed miserable.
Stayed quiet.
Stayed lying.
Stayed cheating.
Stayed emotionally distanced.

We were going to end
regardless,
she just decided to
prolong the pain
so that I could be made
the **villain**
in her once fairytale
relationship.

APOLOGIES & REGRETFUL REMINISCES

Your Person

I just wanted to be able
to hold her,
and stroke her hair,
and trace her face
with my fingertips,
and kiss her slowly
and deep
without feeling guilty
about it.

I missed it.
I missed her.

It felt like home
doing those things,
but only to her.

At least from
what I remember.

I wanted it back.
She was mine,
I had it,
and I let it leave.

I couldn't just do
those actions
with anyone.

I tried.
It was hopeless.

And just not the same
when it's not with
who you truly felt
was **your person**.

I knew she was
my person
back then,
when I had her,
before the "after's"
since then,
and now it's just
a confirmation
that the only person
I could touch like that,
ever,
was her.

Bed

My **bed**,
while vacant,
is warmer
with thoughts of you,
then it is
with her sound asleep,
cuddled up,
with her hand
across my chest.

Heartbreaker

"Mean what you say,
say what you mean."

That's what I
was always taught.
What if I mean it now,
and change my mind later?
Can I do that?
Am I human?

"Mean what you say,
say what you mean."

But I do like her.
Yes, I do think
she's beautiful.

But what if in a week,
or in a month,
I realize that
the beautiful girl,
who is standing
right in front of me,
is meant to stay exactly
where she is right now,
as my friend?
Can I say that?
Am I human?

"Mean what you say,
say what you mean."

I don't regret laying
in one another's arms.
Can I feel that?
Am I human?

The Storm

"Mean what you say,
say what you mean."

The words we spoke
late at night,
were true.
Can I hear that?
Am I human?

"Mean what you say,
say what you mean."

She's the one
who had fallen for me,
and said it was
all my fault.
Can I help that?
Am I human?

They've all taken
so much away from me
with every break
of my heart,
that there's not much
left of me.

But yes,
I am still human,
with a beating heart,
just searching for
true love,
who she has unfairly renamed,
"heartbreaker."

Sacrificed

She had uprooted
three different lives
to my home state.

She elegantly wore
my preference of
hair color,
style,
and length,
without question.

She changed shifts
in her career,
to fit my career's
work schedule.

She tirelessly stayed up
for hours
to quiet my insecurities,
the best that she could.

She left her family.
She left her friends.
She left her plans, behind
to combine her life
with mine.

I'm so sorry for all the
unintentional pain
and stress
I may have caused her,
and for not seeing
until now,
everything she
had **sacrificed.**

Jaws

The first thing I
noticed about her
when she walked
into the room,
were her jaws.

Boxy,
muscular,
clinched,
like an angry pit bull
with quite
the story to tell.

But I later discovered,
that was just a front.
Don't get me wrong,
she was definitely closed off
and quiet
at least in the beginning,
but with a little time,
inappropriate joking,
and persistence on my part,
she would open up
to a select few
from time to time.

I was amongst
those lucky few.
It took some time,
but I got her there.
The place I so longed
for someone to be
with me.
Open, and vulnerable.

We talked for
hours upon hours,
days and nights
on repeat.
We laughed together, a lot.
Her smile told
a thousand stories
and immediately
paralyzed you
in beauty.

You'd get stuck
in a trance,
and sucked in
not wanting it to end,
then lose all
train of thought
Every.
Single.
Time.

We also cried together, a lot.
Me more so than her
because I'm
overly sensitive
and she's more
closed off.
That never stopped me.

It never stopped me from
digging in deep
and from wanting to
discover absolutely everything
about her.

That worked in ways
I never thought it could,
or would.

The Storm

But then,
one night,
we kissed.

It wasn't in her house
and it wasn't in mine,
but man
was it mind-blowing.
Also very unexpected.
I remember it
like it was yesterday.

That kiss led
to many more,
which then led
to vacations,
promises,
introducing the families,
living together,
and eventually,
even to heartbreak.

So that face,
those eyes,
those lips,
they have so
many memories
and stories to tell,
and she keeps them
all lock and key
behind those **jaws.**

Dead

I hurt her.
I hurt her bad.
At first we were
just friends,
everything was great
and the world
was ours.

Too strong
independent women,
dominating in a male
dominant workforce.
She had my back,
and I had hers.

Until the day,
I didn't.

This was almost
four years ago,
and yet,
it still haunts me today
like it did back then.

I was immature,
selfish,
and wrong.

I was mean,
short,
and close-minded.

She never let me
properly apologize.
She wanted absolutely nothing
to do with me,
and I didn't blame her.

The Storm

Back then,
I was the lover,
and she was the fighter.

As time moved forward,
and we grew closer,
there was a phase when
nothing could touch us.

We hit our peak,
and it was amazing.
She had gotten me
to a point of needing her,
craving her,
and there was absolutely
no way of spending
another day in my life
without her in it.

At the top of this
short-lived peak however,
we somehow
role reversed.

She wanted hookups,
and I wanted relationships.

She taught me
how to hook up,
not take everything
so seriously,
and to just live,
one day at a time.

And I taught her
how to put walls down,
and that it was okay
to fall in love.

The problem with us however,
was always communication.
We talked everyday,
and were absolutely inseparable
from one another.

Hell, we even lived together
at one point in our lives.
But whenever it came to talking
about our feelings
and emotions,
we were bad.
Really bad.

I fell for her first,
that's just what I do.
But being friend zoned
or just 'buddies' for so long,
changes you
from the inside out.

I began to make excuses
to myself
for why I should
let her go.

On why I should start,
distancing my heart
from hers.

I thought, fine,
friends it is.

Until a new love interest
trickled into my life.
At this point I was blinded
by what I had hoped
was true love,

that resided in the
New York City dancer.

Of course the friend
wanted to open up
and finally be vulnerable
with me then.
Damn it.

Why did she wait so long
to tell me she loved me?
Why did she wait so long
to tell me how she really felt?
Where could we be today?
Who would we be today?

She was the first,
and still to this day
the only girl to make me feel
physical ways I had never felt.
I wasn't even sure if I
wanted to feel those ways at the time.

Never had I encountered
such a lustful,
aggressive,
passionate love fire
like the one that sparked
between us.

Never had I said
the things I said,
done the things
I had done,
or experienced such a
submissive side in myself,
until I had her.

There is no one
like her.
There will never be anyone
like her,
and that's okay.

How was I such an idiot
not to see what I had
when I had it?

Well now in 2020,
she's back in my life,
unexpected news
to the both of us.

And like the plot twist
to a scary movie,
I'm having to come face to face
with my biggest regret in life.

If I could go back in time
and not hurt her,
if I could go back in time
and not leave her,
if I could go back in time
and not abandon her,
for that stupid pride
on that stupid weekend,
I would in a heartbeat.

If I could go back in time
and keep my promises
and actually be the friend
I swore to her I'd be,
well then maybe,
just maybe,
my heart wouldn't feel shattered

and sinking like the Titanic
in the pit of my stomach
while having to
look her in the eye
and confront her
with all of this now.

Like a soul confessing
it's sins in church,
I find myself falling
to my knees
in a sorrow filled
regretful apology,
completely surrendering
at her mercy.

Today is the day,
because for the first time
in almost four years,
our eyes just met again.

I didn't want to mess it up.
I didn't want to say
the wrong thing.
It was terrifying.

She actually touched me
with a hand shake,
and like a picture flip book,
a jolt of energy rushed
through me.

All memories
came flooding back,
and were carried
straight to my heart
on the backs of butterflies.

She looked good,
but in a way of
missing my best friend.

She had a new glow about her.
That wasn't there before,
and something in me
felt happy for her.

I snapped myself out of it,
and dreadfully
reminded myself,
that almost four years ago,
I hurt her.
I hurt her bad.

And I just pray
for her forgiveness,
and that she doesn't
still wish me **dead.**

War

What's crazy
is that I thought
I could save us.

That there was
something I could do
to win her back
or convince her
to stay.

But there was
never going to be
a saving moment
for us.

The war I was battling
within myself,
was far more
than anything she was
ever going to be able
to handle alone.

She tried,
and I commended her
for that.
But one's own
trust issues,
insecurities,
and ghost
from the past
are ultimately a
two-person battle.

Mine,
for getting over it
and realizing that she
was her own person.
One who I should've given
her own chance too.

And hers,
for reassuring me
that those insecurities
would never return
back to me,
claiming my heart
as it's home.

I see now
that it's too late.
She did her part.

I'm just sorry that
I didn't have the tools
or the armor
to fight in that **war**
with her.

Pride

Sometimes we'd fight
about what later
seemed like
nothing.

Most times
I'd forget mid-fight
what even started it.

I loved her so much,
that I would
unintentionally ignore
her points of view,
and sweep them under
the rug of
unimportance,
just to stop the
arguing.

At the time,
I truly thought I
was helping us,
and that it was
the right thing
for me to do.

It wasn't.
Our fights,
wouldn't stop.
They actually started
getting worse.

I see now,
that those points
she needed to make
in those moments,
they were important
to her.

They were ultimately greater
than the overall
silly moment
that we were even in.

Her points
were important.
They were always,
important.

Her voice
does matter,
always.

I understand that it's
too late for us,
but I want to thank her
for that life lesson,
and opportunity for
personal growth.

This is me,
swallowing my **pride**
and saying,
I'm truly sorry.

Fear

I'm sorry,
because before it got
to what it was
I realized
I wasn't committed fully.

I guess in the back
of my mind,
I really wanted to be.

I wanted her to be the one
who wiped away
all my tears
and washed away
all my fears
from the past.

But if I'm being honest,
I was still scared.

Scared that she would
betray me one day,
before 'forever' came.

Scared she would
see the depths of my scars
under this hopeful smile,
and run
like the rest did.

I wanted to be taught
that committing to her
shouldn't have to be scary.

And instead,
I was left in the dark silence again,
feeling empty of every emotion,
except for the addition,
of one more **fear.**

Slip Away

I find it to be
a bit ironic,
how much we think
we're in control of life.

How we think,
we're in control of our
thoughts,
feelings,
emotions,
and actions.

I would have bet anything
that I'd never talked to her
in any other way,
other than a friend.

Little did I know,
I knew nothing.
She slipped into my life
when I least expected it
and stole my heart
like a burglar
in the middle of
the night.

We had no foundation
to build from,
so how was it that we
were able to grow
so strong and so fast?

Looking back to this day,
I'm reminded of the lesson
I learned that year.

The Storm

How having too many standards,
and being selfish
about what I think is
best for me,
can actually ruin
one of the best things
I ever had.

She stood in front of me
as I turned my head
in the other direction,
and one of the biggest regrets
I still hold to this day,
was letting her
slip away.

Pyramid

There she was,
confused,
looking at me,
while I was looking
at someone else.

How could feelings
be so confusing
when we're all
putting everything
on the table?

A strange bizarre
triangle of confusion
and mixed emotions.

I wanted the other girl
because she knew
what she wanted
and was out and proud.

But I also wanted her,
because unlike the other girl
she taught me
things about myself
I never thought possible.

How does someone
so experienced
stay hidden away
for none to see,
and still able to
teach others about
patience and independence
all while behind the
closed doors of a closet?

The Storm

I was only her everything
once I stopped looking
in her direction,
and that wasn't her fault.

She fell for me,
hard and fast,
but my eyes had already
shifted to another.

I couldn't control the speed
of her emotions about me,
and I couldn't make her
love me,
when I loved her.

The only emotions
I felt responsible for
were my own,
and even that,
I was failing at.

There she was,
looking at me,
looking at someone else,
and none of us,
were happy
in that **pyramid.**

Poison

She said,
she never wanted
to see me again.

She said,
she wasn't attracted
to me anymore,
and that we were nothing
and never would be again.

She said,
the friendship was
dead forever.

She said,
I made her think
unthinkable things
about herself,
and when she told me
what that was,
my heart completely died
inside of me.
Right there,
and in that moment.

I wanted to cry.
I wanted to hug her.
No amount of I'm sorry
could undo what she felt
because of me.

The Storm

Her words that night
were as cold and dark
as the parking lot
we had them in,
and I could tell
I was completely
dead to her.

For what it's worth,
I am so sorry
for letting our love die,
and for being the **poison**
that killed it.

Cry

At this point
I was the worst person
on the planet,
to both her,
and to myself.

Why was she deciding
to tell me this now?
Sitting on the edge of my bed,
confessing feelings
that I tried to dig out of her
several months ago.

She told me,
she was used to
emotionless hookups.
I told her,
I was used to
falling in love.

Neither of us,
seemed very interested
in the others lifestyle,
or outlooks on the matter.

And although there was never
an emotionless moment
between her and I,
there was a moment
of me realizing
I couldn't have her
in the way I wanted
to have her.

The Storm

All of her,
loudly,
outwardly,
proudly,
publicly.

This, with her,
was unfamiliar territory
for me.

I didn't know what to do.
And like all moments
of vulnerability,
the devil swept in
and placed a sweet nothing
in my path
of confusion.

A sweet nothing
that I could be out with,
not even realizing
it was the devil
in disguise.

I had fallen victim
in the midst
of distraction,
and was already
too far gone
when this conversation
had finally surfaced.

I turned my back
on my best friend,
and potential future lover.
On someone who would have
never hurt me.

I knew that then,
and I still know that now.

I was so stupid.
So blind.
And there she was,
standing in the front door frame
of my home,
tears in eyes and
broken heart in hand.
She turned
to face me
and spoke
a thousand words
without ever
moving her lips.

She walked away slowly,
shutting the door
behind her,
and that was
the last time
we saw each other **cry.**

Girls

Over the last decade,
I've gone on so
many dates.
Some planned and
some blind, that were
set up by our friends.

I've shared many
great moments
with these woman and
some of us even
spent the entire night
laughing until we cried.

Heck, some had gotten vulnerable
and deep with me,
and shared emotional tears
over childhood stories and more.

However, there comes a time
in the conversation
where we're sitting there
thinking to ourselves,
'can I truly see spending
the rest of my life
with this person?'

At least, those moments happen
for me anyway.
If we can't see a future in love,
I think it's only fair
to not waste anymore time
on that potential romantic level,
and just agree
to remain friends.

Most of them understood that
and even agreed in a
mutual decision being made.
Some of them
I could tell
really didn't want to
believe it,
and therefore
I unintentionally ended up
hurting them in the process.

That was never my intention
and I hoped we'd stay friends,
but they did not want to stay
long enough for that.

So to the girls who
never made it past a
one-night stand,
and who wanted more
than a friendship with me...

To the girls who had really
taken a leap of faith,
and discussed possibly wanting
a future together...

I'm truly so sorry
that I hurt you.

This is my public apology
and I hope since this
encounter with me,
that you've found your one
true love

and are living your best life
with your best friend
and with the one
God created just for you.

I wish all of you **girls**
the absolute best in life.

Gone

She wasn't my type
until she was.

She taught me things
about my mind
that I had no idea of.

She taught me things
about my body
that I said I would never
let anyone
try and teach me.

There was a dangerous level
of trust and I
enjoyed being vulnerable
in her hands.

She was the first to ever
open me up entirely,
body,
mind,
heart,
and spirit.

There was a different level
of commitment with her,
that I have never had
with anyone before.

There was a level of
vulnerability with her,
that I have never experienced
with anyone before.

I had confidence in her,
and she in me.

The Storm

She took me places,
and showed me states
I had only dreamed of.

She took me places,
physically and emotionally
that I had only thought of.

She made me question
what my 'type' of girl
actually was.

She broke every barrier
I put up,
and every stereotype
I had embedded
in myself.

She was strong,
beautiful,
elegant,
and downright sexy
when we'd go out.

She made me question
everything, everyday.

How could someone
pleasantly torture you one minute,
then curl up in your arms
like a vulnerable kitten
the very next?

She made me question
everything I had ever known
and ever loved.

She taught me things
I didn't even know
I wanted or needed
to experience.
She blew my mind
in more ways than one,
and she would do it,
all at the same time.

I realize now
that not having her
in my life
absolutely sucks.

Breaking her heart
was never my intention,
and if I could go back
and change everything,
I would today
and everyday after.

But I couldn't have
my cake and eat it too.
I messed up.
Plain and simple.

It's been years but
if I'm being honest with myself
I've never really stopped
thinking about her.

She was my best friend,
my confidant,
and someone I really loved
and fully trusted.

The Storm

I had this level of happiness with her
that I've never had with anyone
I've dated, and I realized
that I had blown it.

She wasn't my type
until she was,
and by then,
she was **gone.**

STARTING OVER & MOVING ON

Fly

The love I thought
we had found,
gave the butterflies
in my belly
a new place
to call home.

Being with her
just made sense,
made me feel free,
feel wanted,
feel loved,
fell all the things
I ever dreamed of.

She did what
she needed to do,
to keep me.

She said all the right things,
and threw out promises
during my weakest and
most vulnerable moments
like they were unlimited
to my ears subscription,
to her lips.

As soon as I
spread my wings
and let go
with pure trust in her words,
she scooped me up and
back into her nest of control,
and then clipped
my wings.

No friends.
No calling the family.
Come straight home
after work and
no socializing with
the coworkers.

This is what it became.
This is what we became.

Having full control
over my life and
my decision making,
was an understatement.

But I agreed to this behavior,
because I loved her,
like an idiot.

I had convinced myself
that if I changed into what
she needed me to be,
for her,
that she'd love me enough
to do the same.

She never did,
she never would have,
and she never will
for the poor souls who
come after me.

I didn't take her back
after she left,
because I now know
my self worth.

And honestly honey,
my wings are too beautiful,
and I deserve to **fly**.

Refuel

It eats me up inside,
seeing them
happy together.

It eats me up inside,
knowing she was never
going to change.

It eats me up inside,
knowing that she's playing
the same mind games
with her.

It eats me up inside,
realizing that she's
her own woman,
with her own lessons
to learn.

It eats me up inside,
watching her fake this love
like she did with ours,
and the one before us too.

It eats me up inside,
that I knew the truth
and saw the warnings,
yet still chose to ignore them.

It eats me up inside,
seeing how much time
I wasted on her.
Time I'll never gain back.

She depleted me
of everything,
and I'm an empty tank
that's ready for **refuel.**

Dinner For One

I put her on a
pedestal,
one that she did not
ask to be put on.

I thought I was feeding her
everything she would need
to stay feeling full
and sustained in our
relationship.

Little did I know,
she wasn't hungry,
for me.

She removed herself
from that pedestal
late at night
while my eyes were closed,
so I couldn't see her
run next door and
fill herself
with the sweet sugary calories
from the neighbor.

This time I woke up,
and locked the door.

From now on,
I'll be making **dinner
for one.**

Swallow

All this time,
I've been made to feel
like royalty
sitting at the other end
of this table.

Being trained and
brainwashed,
into thinking I have
the best buffet in town,
right at my fingertips.

The reality of this truth
is that these are
just the scraps.

She had been feeding
me crumbs and garbage
from the dumpster of lies,
and masking the stale taste
of complacency
with it all covered in chocolate and
served on a silver platter.

I never understood why
my stomach would hurt
after she'd feed me another story
of deceit and cover up.

Why I had to get sick
and pass out from crying
after having such a
"pleasant meal" with her.

If she thought that giving
half-ass efforts
and covering them in sugar
was going to sustain me
and make me feel full forever,
then she was sadly mistaken.

Someone else who had
tasted her garbage before,
reached out to me
and unmasked my pallet
to what truth tasted like.

Turns out that she was
the only one who was full of it,
and I was no longer hungry.

It all became way too
hard to **swallow,**
and so I excused myself
from the table,
for the last time.

For Good

I don't understand
myself sometimes.

One minute I'm standing
with a good head
on my shoulders
with the truth
right in front of me.

The very next moment
I'm sitting in a puddle of tears
making excuses for a person
whose mission was to
put me last,
every day.

On my strong days,
she would see me
start to pull away,
start to stand my ground,
and not give in to her.

This is when she would tell me
her most infamous lie,
"I love you".

My ears knew that it
was a lie,
and yet,
by the time the message
reached my heart,
it somehow became
truth inside me.

It's like swimming
in a windy ocean.

The second I find myself
full of strength
and discovering my stride
further and further
away from her toxic island,
she would change direction
of the wind in her favor
by throwing out lines of
"I need you", "I love you", and "I want you",
forcing my rhythmic swim
straight back to her.

I'm done allowing this to happen
time and time again.

So today,
I'm putting in my ear plugs,
blocking out the lies in which
I know to be true,
and I'm swimming away
from her toxic island,
for good.

Why Not

She told me that
it was so hard
for her to talk to me,
yet she so easily
talked to her every night
behind my back.

She told me she
didn't have the time
to go on trips with me,
yet she so easily
bought a plane ticket
to another state,
to go see her for
the entire weekend.

She told me she
didn't want to have sex,
because she was too tired
and stressed from work,
yet she so easily
found the strength
to give the mistress
every once of her energy.

I deserve someone who
wants me,
the way I want them.

Life is far too short
to wait.

So, **why not** do that
for myself now?

Yeah, that actually sounds amazing,
and I'm officially done.

Victim

My mind,
my heart,
and my body
were open temples to her
at her leisure.

Yet she treated it like
something she needed to
break into and
rob from in the
middle of the night.

It was hers,
for as long as she wanted it,
but once claimed,
the thrill was over for her.

She needed the chase
like a cat needs a mouse.

She needed the hunt
like a lion needs a gazelle.

The fun for her was over,
so she moved on to the next.

She quickly realized that the game
she played on me,
she was now the lead character of
in the new girl's game.

On hands and knees
she tried to crawl back
knocking on the door
of the heart
that was once hers.

The Storm

The door looks different,
because it is.

It's been replaced.

Thicker,
stronger, and
padlocked shut.

This door is not
voice activated,
so she can save the
apologies,
for her next **victim.**

I Wasn't

How was she able
to do that?

Treat me like shit
and push me to the brink
of leaving
because I knew
I deserved better.

Then was able to turn it
around on me
as if it was all my fault.

People don't get to pick
and choose when they decide
to be nice.

She didn't get to decide
the days she felt like
loving me.

We were either all in,
or we were all out.

I was so tired of feeling crazy
when I knew I wasn't.

I was so tired of being made to feel
like the bad guy in all of it
when I knew I wasn't.

I was so tired of feeling used,
abused,
and made to feel unworthy,
when I knew I wasn't.

The Storm

I think she truly believed
that I was going to stay there,
and continue suffering in that
toxic relationship with her.

Well,
I wasn't.

Out Of Sight Out Of Mind

I need to keep her blocked,
on everything.

Don't call,
don't text,
don't message me
on social media
in any way,
shape, or form.

I need time to heal.
I need time to remember
and to remind myself
why this needs to happen.

Why I need to move on
because she's no good
for me.

With her in arms reach,
I keep forgetting
that she's no longer
mine.

With her only a click away,
I keep forgetting that I
shouldn't call her.

With her on my newsfeed,
I keep forgetting that I
shouldn't heart that status,
or laugh at that meme.

I don't want to keep forgetting,
so where I need her,
is **out of sight out of mind.**

Curse

For so long,
I forgave myself
for the things I
did not say,
for the things I
had not done,
and for the person
she made me believe
I was.

I completely lost
my identity while
with her.

And I see now,
how silly I must have looked
to others.

Others who cared about me
and said for months
that I had the wool
pulled over my eyes.

That she had blinded me
from the truth,
and manipulated me
into always thinking
I was in the wrong for
speaking up.

My eyes have been
revealed to the truth,
and I thank God,
I'm finally free
from her **curse**.

Just Getting Started

'Don't worry dear,
you'll find them,
it's just a matter of time.'

It must be getting
old by now?

People telling you that
your true love
is out there
waiting for you.

Or what about this one,
'they're fixing themselves now
to be better for you,
they're just not ready yet.'

Or has anyone fed you the line,
'patience is a virtue,
it'll all happen when
the time is right.'

But all we want
is love.

We want it now or
probably tomorrow
at the latest.

Why does it always seem like
everyone is finding love,
but us?

Well don't worry dear,
you and I are in
the same boat,

The Storm

drowning in these
love stories together.

I say we work on us,
for now,
and learn to be happy,
alone.

At least for
a little while.

We need to stop being so
hard on ourselves.

We're only setting ourselves up
for more disappointment.

Every journey
is a lesson.

Lets take it by the hand,
study it,
become it.

And whether we're in
our twenties,
fifties,
or eighties,
we're still young
and there's still time,
because at the end of
all of this,
this precious little thing
called life
on this precious little thing
called Earth,
well, it's nowhere
near the end.
Oh honey,
how we're **just
getting started.**

Daily Dose

You get to a point in life
where you realize just what
toxicity looks like.

You realize what
narcissists sound like.

You realize what
liars taste like.

The lies roll off their lips
as fast as ice cream
melts in the sun.

They can't help it.
It's just who they are.

You start believing
the stories
they've concocted in
their heads
and have planted in
your thoughts.

You start thinking
everything's,
your fault.

That every argument
that leads them to
wanting to leave you,
is because of something
YOU, said or did.

Suddenly when they
belittle you,
and talk down to you
like you're nothing,
that's YOUR fault.

When they had to
put hands on you
that one time,
and then that other time,
oh and the time after that too,
again, that's YOUR fault.

Well let me tell you something
Honey,
you get to a point in life
where you realize
your self worth.

It just clicks,
and you begin to see that,
none of that,
ever,
was your fault.

Put your foot down,
and stand up for yourself.

Stop letting them
come back in
when THEY choose
to leave.

Stop letting them
come back in,
when you've already
rightfully
gotten rid of them.

Especially stop,
letting them win.
They're not winning,
not anymore.

Unfortunately,
there is no medication
to fix their problem,
but there is for yours.

So stop allowing them
to spread onto you,
their **daily dose** of
toxic cancerous behavior,
once and for all.

You deserve better.

Second Chances

Do you believe in
second chances?

Do you believe
in giving,
second chances?

Were your answers
the same,
or did you hesitate on one?

Giving someone who's
hurt you in the past
a second chance,
is a very personal decision.

For some,
they realize their partners worth,
and they consciously choose to
never hurt them again.

For me,
with every second chance
I gave,
they completely took
advantage of it.

They took advantage of
my grace and kindness,
and inevitably
hurt me worse
the second time around.

It's a risky move,
gambling your heart.

You have to ask yourself,
will this be worth it?

I tell myself
time and time again,
'you've done this before.
You've been here, remember?
What's going to make this time
any different
from the past?'

Sometimes I feel like
I'm setting myself up
for failure
with second chances.

Every time I do,
I put blinders on
because honestly I'm too scared
to see the truth
for what it is.

We get hurt
over and over again
by our own doing,
and then blame others
for not warning us
that it was coming.

Even though they
spelled it out,
and completely in
black and white,
a dozen times.

I've finally realized,
for my long term
happiness,
no more **second chances.**

Hypocrite

Why do we feel so justified
to give advice
on other's relationships,
but then choose to
ignore the red flags
in our own?

When a friend speaks up
to try and help out of love,
you may start to think,
'maybe it's not actually red?
maybe it's orange,
or from this angle,
it kind of looks like a
shade of pink?
But no,
it's definitely not red.'

We get defensive
and think to ourselves,
'what does it matter?
MY relationship
is nowhere near as bad
as theirs,
so I'll just keep
giving my unasked for opinion
on their situation,
and ignoring their opinions
on mine.

They don't know anything.
They act like they can see
something in MY relationship
that I can't see.

I ALWAYS know what's going on
in MY relationship,
and they should just
mind their own business.'

We always think that from where
we're standing, that we can see all
of everyone else's issues going on
in their relationships.

However, we never take ownership
to look closer into our own.

Why is that?

We think,
'how dare them to
assume that they know what we
talk about behind closed doors.'

We gossip
amongst each other,
'who do they think they are?
How dare them say that
about the woman I love!'

Instead of remembering
that this IS coming from
someone who loves you.

We get cocky,
and say that we don't
need to hear everything they
talk about in their relationship
behind closed doors,
to be able to see that they're
not going to last forever.

The Storm

Well, the way that you think
that you can see things
that they don't,
that works both ways.

The way that you feel
privileged to speak up
and give your opinion on others,
especially when it's not asked for,
or the way you try to
defend your relationship
because you have it's
best interests at heart,
well, that also works both ways.

Stop making excuses
for the red flags
in your own relationship
when they start to
reveal themselves.

If you do choose to
ignore them,
don't get mad at the friends
who tried to warn you
when you get hurt again.

Be a friend to your friends,
and to yourself.
Not a **hypocrite.**

Leave

When their behavior
doesn't change,
yet they expect you to
on a daily basis...

When they request all facts
and details upfront,
yet they lied to your face
every chance they got...

When you choose to
withhold information from
your children,
about what is actually happening
behind closed doors,
only to protect their youth,
and their hearts from
being broken,
yet the other party chooses to
use them as pawns
and play them against you...

Honey, you're in a
narcissistic relationship.

One that will never change,
and only progressively
get worse over time.

For the best interest
of yourself,
and your children,
it's time to **leave.**

Pros And Cons

There are always
three sides,
to every story.

Yours,
theirs,
and the truth.

There is always good
on both sides,
and there is always bad
on both sides.

Always weigh them out.

Like a wave in the ocean,
out of nowhere,
forms this huge rush
of energy towards you.

They want back in.

They're sorry, and they
want another chance.

You think to yourself,
'why would I date someone
who's already proven
to be untrustworthy
with the key to my heart?
They've lost it once before.'

You also think,
'why not just start fresh
with someone new and give
someone else the chance to
prove themselves
worthy of my love?'

And this is where
the weighing happens.

The pros to dating an ex,
is that they already
know you.

What makes you smile,
laugh,
feel loved,
and how your brain works.

The con to dating your ex
is that they already
know you.

They know every button,
what it does,
and when to push it
to only benefit themselves.

The pros to dating someone new
is that it's a blank slate.

There's no damage done,
and only tons of clear air
and open space to build trust
and a happy and healthy foundation
of a friendship on.

The Storm

The con to dating someone new,
is simply having to
start all over again,
when in fact,
you may not even
want to anymore.

The decision of
letting anyone in close to
your heart
is incredibly hard,
but always remember that
your gut and your heart,
are never wrong.

Remember to weigh out
all your **pros and cons**,
and always,
listen to yourself.

Listen to that beautiful heart.

Once you're in tune
with your intuition,
you can never go wrong.

Body Language

There are going to
come times in life
where your brain
either doesn't want to work,
or just feels
too overwhelmed
to think.

In these life moments,
decisions still need
to be made.

When you can't think
of the right thing to do,
let your body
speak for you.

Those hairs
on the back of
your neck,
when they stand,
they're talking.

Those lumps
in the back of
your throat,
when you can't swallow them,
they're talking.

Those knots
in the pit of
your stomach,
when they tangle,
they're talking.

The Storm

So when your brain
is too overwhelmed
with the abuse
you've had to endure
over the years,
listen to your
body language,
because it just might be
what helps you escape.

Think, That Way

Your heart is enough.
Your love is enough.
Your brain is enough.
Your body is enough.

Things that I
forget to tell myself
when yet another
comes in and promises
me 'forever.'

Just to later be told
in their actions,
that I am in fact,
not enough.

Maybe they were just
the wrong person?
And the next,
and the next,
and the next.

What is so wrong with me,
that no one
wants to stay?

Your heart is enough.
One day, someone will
fully appreciate it.

Your love, is enough.
One day, someone won't
take it for granted.

The Storm

Your brain, is enough.
One day, someone will
love you without trying
to manipulate it.

Your body, is enough.
One day, someone won't
abuse you,
not physically,
and not emotionally.

And to them,
that right person,
you will undoubtedly
be flawless too.

Sometimes I have to dig deep
to be able to remind
myself of this,
because I was not created
and put on this Earth
to **think, that way.**

2:00 A.M. Thoughts

It's 2:00 a.m.
and I am in bed
alone.

This is the first time,
I'm not sad about it.

I think I'm going to
call out today.

I think I'm going to
sleep in today.

I think I'm going to
cook myself a real meal tonight
and I'm going to enjoy it
in the presence of
my own company.

I think I'm going to do
whatever I feel like
doing today,
and what I feel like
doing today,
is loving myself.

I definitely could get used to
these feelings,
and these
2:00 a.m. thoughts.

First Impressions

I'm the type of person who
has such a wide variety
of personalities,
that I can get along
with just about any crowd.

That becomes a problem for me
once it is mixed with my mentality
of thinking that everyone
wants to be my friend.

I'm gullible and
vulnerable enough
to believe the lies
as they're happening
right in front of my face.

I try to see the good
in everyone.

I want to believe
that all people,
are good.

I allow myself to be
convinced over how people
first display themselves as.

Sometimes when I see red flags,
I ignore them.

Other times when I've
gotten stepped on,
or thrown under the bus,
I forgive too quickly.

You would think
as an adult,
after you experience
the pain of touching
the hot stove,
you wouldn't reach back out
for a second round.

Yet here I am,
forgiving and taking those back
who have hurt me before.

Once people show true colors,
that's it, I'm out.

I am done allowing people
to play me,
throw dirt on my name,
spit on my integrity,
or play me like a simple
brainless pawn
in their little mind game.

No more second chances.

From now on,
I'm listening to my gut,
and relying solely
on **first impressions.**

Which Shoulder

The devil is on
one shoulder
and whispers in my ear,
while God's angel is on
the other,
saying the complete opposite.

I know which shoulder
I want to always listen to,
but sometimes the devil
is just so obnoxiously loud.

One side knows better,
the other side does not.

One side is confident,
the other side is not.

One side knows
what I deserve,
the other side
does everything to prevent me
from having that.

One side tells me to leave,
and the other side
convinces me that staying
is the only option.

One side reminds me
of the abuse and tells me
it's time to move on,
and the other side says
suck it up and that I
won't find better if I do.

Lindsey Kay Atkinson

I know **which shoulder**
I will always listen to,
and that's why
I'm leaving her today.

Happily Ever After

I discovered
something very odd
by accident one day.

That every girl
I've ever dated,
is still with the person
they left me for.

I find that odd,
yet very intriguing.

What about me
are all these women gaining,
that allows the very next person
they date after me,
to become the one?

At first,
I looked at it in a
negative light,
like I was cursed
from some witch
in some far away
fantasy land,
who put me under
some spell
of heartbreak.

That with every girl
I kissed,
I'd be heartbroken by,
and then her true
knight in shining armor
would be close behind,
to save her.

But then I found God.

And as I bring myself
back down to earth,
I start to wonder…

Are these women
finding true love,
because of me?

Am I showing them
what it feels like
to be truly loved
for the first time?

How painless a
relationship can be
when they settle for
hugs and kisses
instead of fist?

How to become addicted
to the words 'I love you' and
'Baby you mean the world to me'
instead of a
needle in their arm
or white substances
on their nose?

How to love their children
in the most positive and
supportive ways they can,
even when they thought
they couldn't possibly
love them anymore
then they already did?

I showed them,
that they could.

I showed them,
how to be heard and
not ignored or
thrown to the waste side
as if their opinions and
voices didn't matter.

How to make them realize
that they are worthy and
that their life is in fact
worth living.

Sure, I always end up single
and heartbroken,
but look at how many souls
I'm helping find
happiness.

Now I look at it as
more of a superpower.

So basically,
when you really
break it down,
there's no real downside
to dating me.

If we work, then great,
I'm your soulmate and
we finally found each other.

But know that if we don't,
I've at least used
my superpower
on another soul by
showing you your worth,
and have groomed you
in preparation of finding
your **happily ever after**, next.

Me

Why?
Why do all of them
come back,
and do it so quietly?

When they clearly make the
biggest scene
on their way out?

They walk away angry,
hateful,
and make everyone believe
that I'm the bad guy,
I guess to,
help ease the heartbreak
on their side of this.

I guess it's that they
finally realize
what I meant when I said
they were stuck with me
forever.

I didn't mean physically.
I'm not possessive.

No, what I meant was
that I've imprinted
on their hearts.

I'm burned into their
memories forever.

All the good
I did for them.

All the good
I was to them.

None of it will be
easily forgotten.

They're realizing how
weak they feel
without me.

That's because they
took advantage of my strength
when they had it.

They're realizing how
empty they feel
without me.

That's because they
took advantage of my love
when they had it.

They're realizing how
unhappy they are
without me.

That's because they
took advantage of my joy in life
when they had it.

It's for all these same reasons
that they keep trying
to come back.

Well the door to my heart
is forever closed to them,
and I've fallen in love
with someone new.

That's someone's name,
is **me**.

Feet On The Ground

I wouldn't say that I'm scared
to love again,
I would say that
I'm hesitant.

I've realized in my
past relationships,
that there's a pattern.

Girl meets girl.
They fall in love.
Then they promise each other
the world.

They jump in blindly
like a professional diver
assuming the pool is full.

Well, the pool is full.

But it's full of lies,
deceit,
anger,
pain,
heartbreak,
misery,
and eventually
break up.

They knows this,
they're warned of this,
but they're in love,
and so they dive in anyway.

Over the years,
I've come to learn
that I'm more of a bungee jumper
kind of lover.

I could blame who I date,
on bad luck, or a
broken picker.

Or,
I could take full responsibility
for who I choose to date,
and when.

Like a bungee jumper,
I take my time
getting to the platform.

I ensure that my equipment
is safe and secure.

I step up,
take a deep breath,
and jump.

This is where I mess up,
every time.

I jump,
blindly with little to no protection
around my heart.

I jump,
with little to no security.

The Storm

Love and lust team up and
push me from behind
when I least expect it.

But I go with it anyway.

The rush of the free fall,
the adrenaline of falling in love,
takes my breath away,
until suddenly,
it stops.
Like flipping to the last page
of your favorite book,
it's just over.

And here I go,
ripped away into a backwards
time warp of emotions,
watching the flashbacks
and memories of everything good,
happening in reverse,
as the destination that my
eyes and heart
are fixated on,
become smaller and smaller,
and harder to reach.

Here I am,
back on the platform,
checking my gear again
and preparing for
my next jump.

It's truly like a nightmare
you can't wake up from.

I no longer want
to have nightmares,
but rather,
I crave to dream.

I no longer want
to be a bungee jumper,
but rather,
I wish to learn how to
skydive.

I want time to
study myself in the hangar,
and be able to build up
the confidence
to enter into this new chapter
of my life,
and bored the plane,
completely alone.

I want to fly high,
independently and solo,
and give myself the opportunity
to grow brave
while no one else
is watching.

I want to reach a peek
in the journey,
and then be tested on
what I've learned.

I want to be scared.
I want to feel every butterfly
and every ounce of
nervousness along the way.

The Storm

I want to stick my neck out
with eyes closed,
and feel God's presence
on my face,
in the wind.

And I want to know
in my heart,
and in my soul,
that when I CHOOSE to let go,
that I won't be falling into
the unknown again.

I don't want to
blindly fall anymore.
I want to glide,
with eyes open wide.

I wish to feel nothing
but peace and serenity
without the fear of losing time
with every mile
that passes by.

I wish to gain knowledge and insight
along the way,
that allows me to know for sure
of when to pull the ripcord,
and reassurance that
when I do,
it's because it's the
perfect time
to slow things down.

And with this insight,
courage,
knowledge,
patience,
confidence,
security,
and readiness I'll gain,
I wish to glide down easily
and into the arms of
the woman God created
just for me.

I'm ready to find the girl,
who can't wait to keep,
my **feet on the ground.**

Storms

My patience
is a problem.

I want so badly
to find love
that I try to find it
in people for all the
wrong reasons.

Whether they've ever
been married,
had kids,
want to get married,
or ever want to have kids.

All of these questions
are irrelevant when it
comes to building
our foundation.

My relationship foundations
have always had
cracks in them,
and they inevitably end up
crumbling to dust,
before we're ever able
to really get started.

That's because they're
rushed and moved into,
before the cement dries.

And although these questions
are of importance to me,
they hold no weight
to stability.

I need to worry less
about the future,
and focus more
on the present.

I want to one day
marry my best friend,
and I can't do that
until I date someone with a
built-up friendship
of trust and security,
and who has a passion to
want to build a sturdy foundation
with me,
that will withstand even the strongest
of **storms**.

I know true love exists for me,
I'm just waiting for the calm after the storm.

DEAR READER

Thank you so much for choosing to spend time in your day to be with me.
It means the world to me that you chose my poems to read. I hope that you can't resonate with my pains and heartaches, for no one should ever have to endure pain like such.

However, if you unfortunately can resonate with this level of pain and heartbreak that I have, I hope I was able to bring you some peace in knowing that you're not in this alone.

If you enjoyed reading this book, I would be absolutely honored to hear from you. They say the best way to show an author your appreciation is to express and share your thoughts and feelings.

I would love to know the thoughts and stories streaming through you while you were reading about my pain, and how each and every one of you feel after reading it. If you take a brief moment to leave a short review at the retailer's site where you purchased this from, I would be more grateful than you could possibly imagine.

Thank you readers, for allowing me a safe space in your heart to express the pain, heartbreak, depression, and loneliness I've endured over the years.
It's for people like us that I keep pushing forward. We deserve true love, and I'll fight for us forever.

For your continued love and support on my platforms, I am grateful beyond measure. May God bless each and everyone of you.

ACKNOWLEDGEMENTS

I have to first address the sincerest of gratitude to God, who has never led me astray. It is through His mighty power at work within me, that I was able to accomplish infinitely more than I thought to ask. I wouldn' know where to step next without His loving guidance and understanding that even through the valley's, there's beauty and growth to be learned.

Thanks also to my entire loving family. Specifically my Mom and Grandmother, who have always emotionally, prayerfully, and sometimes even financially supported my dreams in coming true.

I am also grateful for the continued support and enthusiasm from my friends all over the globe who stayed up all hours of the day to hear my writings as they were being written.

Finally, I am also grateful and humbled to have such an amazing fan base from youtube, who have patiently and selflessly understood the passion that I'm following, from temporarily leaving the screen, for the pages with wanting to become a writer.

It's because of all of you, I found the courage to step outside my comfort zone, speak up on the topics I've never been brave enough too, and to leap forward with eyes closed and arms open to do the very thing I've been postponing for years…...write a book.

I hope that everyone reading this can resonate with my poems, even if only one, and that it brings you peace in healing and reminding you that you are never alone.

ABOUT THE AUTHOR

Lindsey Kay Atkinson is an author, poet, and social media influencer who is devoted to making an impact through both her writing and her YouTube videos.

Lindsey was born and raised in Maryland where she still resides. Lindsey attended four different schools throughout her elementary and middle school years, becoming very familiar with the life of having many friends from many different backgrounds.

After graduating from Old Mill Senior High School in 2010, she attended Anne Arundel Community College where she played basketball and graduated with her Associates degree in transfer studies, with a focus on Deaf Culture and ASL interpreting.

With many connections from across the states, her following on YouTube for making music video's in sign language, continued to grow making her most popular video reaching over a million views in only a couple of weeks.

Lindsey now hopes to join her writing passion and her YouTubing passion onto one platform with the same goal in mind...changing the lives of others with encouraging and supportive messages to uplift the soul.

Lindsey spends her days writing and working on many projects with her beloved german Shepherds, Chopper and Letty, always dropping toys on her notebooks and resting their heads on her writing arm. She hopes to continue exploring expression and the art of healing through poetry, and the art of music in sign language, for years to come.

BOOKS COMING SOON

The Calm
The Rainbow

You can contact Lindsey through **lindseykayatkinson.com**
and find her on these platforms:

Facebook: Lindsey Atkinson
Instagram: @lindseyatkinson3_poetry
YouTube: @lindseyatkinson3
Twitter: @lindsey_shay
Pinterest: @lindseyatkinson3

Want to send fan mail or become pen pals with Lindsey?
She loves receiving letters from fans and
followers, and she will write you back!
Just add a pre-stamped envelope inside with your letter,
and she'll write you back the same week!

You can send them to:
Lindsey Atkinson
PO Box 87
Severn MD, 21144

If you've ever felt heartbreak, depression,
confusion, fear, anxiety, sadness
or loneliness after a breakup,
know that you're not alone.

In order to heal,
we must first acknowledge the pain,
and address the wound.

So this is for all my other
hopeless romantics out there
who've lived through the experience
of putting your fragile heart
in the wrong hands,
one too many times...

Made in the USA
Middletown, DE
16 August 2023

36821972R00149